Group Captain Douglas Steuart Bader
C.B.E., D.S.O., D.F.C., was educated at St Edward's School, Oxford, and the R.A.F. College, Cranwell. He was commissioned in June 1930, and posted to 23 Fighter Squadron. On 14 December 1931, he crashed in a Bristol Bulldog single-seater fighter losing both legs as a result. In May 1933 he was invalided from the R.A.F. and in June joined the Shell Company.

In November 1939, he rejoined the Royal Air Force. His promotion was rapid and his success spectacular. Starting with his retired rank of Flying Officer, he became Flight Lieutenant in April 1940, a Squadron Leader in June, and a Wing Commander in March 1941.

Bader's official score was 22½ German aircraft destroyed. On 9 August 1941 he was brought down over France and became a prisoner of war. After escaping for 24 hours from his hospital in St. Omer, he was taken to Germany under heavy escort. In his first twelve months as a prisoner, he was transferred through six P.O.W. camps from two of which he made abortive attempts to escape. In August 1942 he arrived at Colditz where he remained until his release by the U.S. First Army on 15 April 1945.

Douglas Bader retired from the Royal Air Force as a Group Captain in 1946 and rejoined the Shell International Petroleum Company. He retired from Shell in 1969. He is now a member of the Board of the Civil Aviation Authority and still flies his own small aeroplane. He has spent the whole of his working life in aviation and has no intention of stopping.

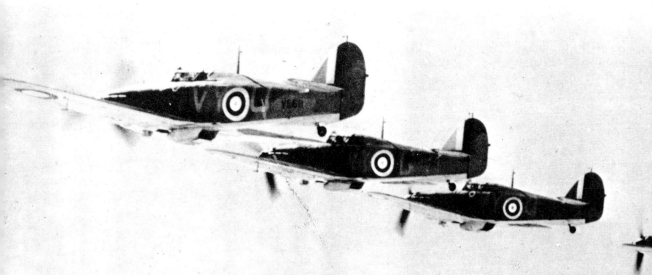

Contents

DOUGLAS BADER
FIGHT FOR THE SKY

The Story of the Spitfire
and the Hurricane by
Group Captain Douglas Bader
CBE DSO DFC

with special contributions and help from:

Group Captain Sir Max Aitken
DSO DFC

Air Chief Marshal Sir Harry
Broadhurst
GCB KBE DSO DFC AFC

Air Commodore A. C. Deere
DSO OBE DFC

Group Captain H. S. L. Dundas
DSO DFC

Wing Commander D. Gillam
DSO DFC AFC

Air Vice Marshal J. E. Johnson
CB CBE DSO DFC

Wing Commander P. B. Lucas
DSO DFC

Air Vice Marshal M. Lyne
CB AFC

Special research by John Frayn Turner
Designed by Paul Watkins
Photo research by John Moore

Fontana/Collins

First published by Sidgwick & Jackson 1973
First published in Fontana 1975
© 1973 text by Douglas Bader
© 1973 design and artwork by Sidgwick and Jackson Limited
Printed in Great Britain by William Collins Sons & Co. Ltd, Glasgow
Origination by Morrison and Gibb Ltd Edinburgh

The title page shows Hurricanes flying in formation (1940)

CONDITIONS OF SALE: This book is sold subject to the condition that it shall not, by way of trade or otherwise, be lent, re-sold, hired out or otherwise circulated without the publisher's prior consent in any form of binding or cover other than that in which it is published and without a similar condition including this condition being imposed on the subsequent purchaser.

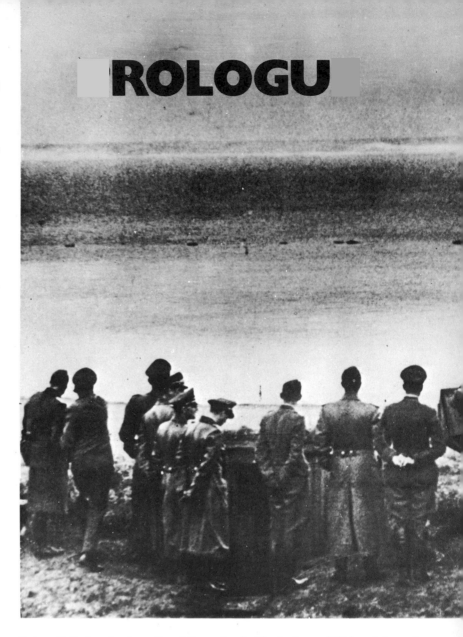

PROLOGUE

I was delighted when Lord Longford, Chairman of Sidgwick and Jackson, London, asked me to write the story of the Spitfire and Hurricane. My memories went straight back to June 1940. The Germans had by then conquered Poland, Norway, Denmark, Holland, Belgium, and France. The British people stood alone, separated from enemy-occupied Europe by twenty-one miles of blessed English Channel. Those immortal words which Shakespeare put into the mouth of the dying John of Gaunt—in Richard II:

'This royal throne of kings, this sceptred isle . . .
This precious stone set in the silver sea,
Which serves it in the office of a wall,
Or as a moat defensive to a house . . .'

'A moat . . . which the Germans
could not attempt to cross
without first defeating the
Royal Air Force—in particular
the Spitfire and the Hurricane'
(picture shows Goering and
staff gazing across Channel in
1940)

comforted many of us when we reflected that the English Channel was indeed a moat which provided an insuperable tank obstacle which the Germans could not attempt to cross without first defeating the Royal Air Force—in particular the Spitfire and the Hurricane.

I recall as though yesterday a scene in the Mess at Kirton-in-Lindsay to which 222 Squadron (Spitfires) had returned in early June after Dunkirk. We were all standing around the ante-room at lunchtime listening to the B.B.C. news. The announcement came over the air that the French Government had capitulated. Tubby Mermagen, the Commanding Officer of 222 Squadron in which I was a Flight Commander, said: 'Thank God, now we're on our own.' He expressed the feelings of us all.

'A plume of black smoke from the burning oil tanks at Shell Haven . . . stains the blue summer sky . . .'

Another memory that came back vividly was of the first time I led a squadron into battle—it was against a horde of German bombers, sixty to a hundred of them flying at 17,000 feet in perfect formation. We were in the ideal position, up-sun and above them.

There were nine of us Hurricanes. Suddenly, I was angry. 'Who the hell do these Huns think they are, flying like this in their bloody bombers covered with iron crosses and swastikas over our country?' We were flying in sections of three in line astern, exactly above the Germans.

I told the two sections behind that I would dive to attack the front of the enemy formation and they would follow immediately after my section had made contact. It worked perfectly. As we hit them, the leading German bombers and their twin-engined Messerschmitt fighter escorts banked away to right and left,

which disrupted the ones behind them, so the entire formation was broken into separate units turning south and making for home, pursued and in some cases being shot down by Hurricanes. Later in the evening we heard to our great satisfaction that other British fighters had knocked down more of this formation as they went south. It was a satisfactory first outing.

I recall also one morning during a mêlée in the sky, sighting a German bomber which seemed a good target. I was closing from behind when some instinct made me look up to see a Spitfire above me diving near-vertically at the German. As I throttled back watching, the Spitfire hit the enemy exactly in the centre, where wings and fuselage meet. The bomber sort of folded up round the fighter and the whole lot caught fire and drifted apparently quite slowly downwards just like a screwed up ball of paper set alight and thrown from a cliff. Clearly the Spitfire pilot was diving to attack some other enemy and did not see the one he hit.

Indeed memories come flooding back ... two Hurricanes converging to attack the same German bomber, each pilot concentrating on his target, oblivious of the sky around him. They touch and a wing breaks off to float away like an autumn leaf from a tree. One pilot bales out and lives to fight again tomorrow and all the rest of the days the battle lasted.

A German bomber diving and zooming all over the sky. A closer look reveals what appears to be a weight swinging some feet below the tail. It is one of the crew whose parachute got wrapped round the tail as he baled out. There is no one in the cockpit.

That same morning, in that same sky, another German attempts to leave his dying bomber. As far as the watching Hurricane pilot can see, his parachute pack gets caught half-way out and the man is held against the fuselage with the parachute inside and him outside. A brave companion frees him and both sail down to captivity.

A plume of black smoke from the burning oil-tanks at Shell Haven, on the Thames Estuary, stains the blue summer sky to a height of 10,000 feet. A large formation of Germans has been broken up by Spitfires and Hurricanes and the usual aftermath of personal combats is going on all over the place between 15,000 and 10,000 feet. I am lining up an enemy in my sights when I look in my mirror to see the yellow nose of an Me 109 lining me up in his. I turn away left just in time; but not quite. A stream of bullets arrives in the right hand side of the cockpit frightening me out of my wits, but causing no serious damage. I straighten up to see my 109 go past with a Hurricane on his tail. As I look, the Messerschmitt goes into a steepening dive emitting white smoke and flame. It disappears into the black smoke from Shell Haven. The German had not looked behind before he started shooting at me.

'. . . two fighters, born of British genius, produced by British craftsmen, and, in the event, sustained by the whole British nation'

Opposite: The author, 1940

There were strange, unforgettable sights in the sky over south-east England in those far-off Battle of Britain days.

Winston Churchill's historic remark about the Few made us proud, and we loved him for it. But the Battle was not won only by us in the sky. It was won by every man and woman in this country. We had the good job, we could fight back. They were on the ground building fighters to replace the ones we lost; when their factories were bombed they went on producing them under bridges and in the open. They did not stop. The ground crews of the Royal Air Force worked round the clock to keep our aeroplanes in trim. The Operations rooms were on watch night and day. The Ops Room at Detling received a direct hit with the near total loss of all the men and women inside.

The voluntary services, air-raid wardens, firemen, doctors, hospital workers, engineers, police, shopkeepers, dockers, the Observer Corps, the whole community sustained us fighter pilots with their courage.

We were their representatives in the air. Meanwhile our wonderful Merchant Navy, escorted by the Royal Navy, brought to all of us in our beleaguered island the necessities of life and the wherewithal to continue our struggle for survival. The East End of London with its docks received heavy attention from the Luftwaffe but the spirit of the Cockney was unbreakable.

I shall never forget a picture in the newspapers of a German bomber, minus its tail, diving into a tobacconist shop on the corner of Victoria Station. It was an incredible shot and showed the enemy aeroplane about 200 feet from the ground. A subsequent photograph depicted the shop in ruins with the grinning proprietor standing outside. In front of him on the pavement was a trestle table with some packets of cigarettes upon it together with a cardboard notice on which was pencilled 'Business as usual'. That was the spirit which won the Battle of Britain. The pilot's account of shooting down that particular enemy is in this book.

I make no apology for saying all this in a book about the Spitfire and Hurricane. It is part of the story of these two matchless fighters, born of British genius, produced by British craftsmen and, in the event, sustained by the whole British nation.

Memories crowd the mind, but the one which dominates all others is that of the British people at bay, united and unconquerable, in our island kingdom.

This book is far more than a collection of my reminiscences and the story of the Battle of Britain. Combat reports of pilots support the narrative, while accounts of campaigns have been included from chaps who were there.

Above all, the story of the Spitfire and the Hurricane is the story of Britain's war. They fought on every battle front, from the Arctic wastes of northern Russia to the tropical jungles of the Far East; from the green of Europe to the brown of Northern Africa.

They flew high, they flew low; they were catapulted off ships (the Sea Hurricane); they flew off aircraft carriers (the Seafire); they were adapted to most military and many naval tasks. In the Western Desert campaign against the German Afrika Korps with its redoubtable leader, General Rommel, Spitfires were used to escort low-flying cannon Hurricanes which created havoc among the armoured vehicles and tanks of the enemy. In Europe, during the closing stages of the war, cannon-firing Spitfires and Hurricanes devastated retreating enemy columns on road and railway lines. They provided the R.A.F., Royal Navy, and Allied air forces with almost unlimited variations in armament and range. At various times both these remarkable fighters were adapted to carry bombs or rockets.

Except for one brief period in 1942, when the German Focke-Wulf 190 mastered the Spitfire Vb, this superlative fighter dominated the skies over Europe and North Africa. I have often wondered who the genius was who christened it Spitfire. It was a name that resounded round the free world in those dark years of Hitler's tyranny, and perfectly symbolized the mood of Britain's defiance.

I IN FLIGHT AND IN
Personal impressions of the fighters

In 1933 the front-line fighters of the Royal Air Force had been biplanes with fixed undercarriages, tailskids, two-bladed fixed-pitch wooden propellers, and no blind-flying instruments; they carried two machine guns firing between the propeller blades (if you were lucky) by means of an interrupter gear. Maximum speed was 180–200 m.p.h.

At the end of November 1939, I was posted as a Flying Officer (the rank I held on retirement in May 1933) to the Central Flying School, Upavon, for a refresher course on modern types of aircraft.*

Now, modern types consisted of low-wing monoplanes, with retractable undercarriages, wing flaps, constant-speed variable-pitch propellers, blind-flying instruments and radio telephony. None of these things had existed when I crashed in 1931.

I was posted to No. 19 Squadron (Spitfires) in February 1940. The Commanding Officer was Squadron Leader Geoffrey Stephenson, an exact contemporary of mine. We were close friends from Cranwell days. In 1939 there was no such thing as a two-seater Hurricane or Spitfire. You were instructed on an advanced training aeroplane called a Miles Master. It was a two-seater in which the instructor sat behind you. This Master was nothing like a Hurricane or Spitfire, for it had a wide undercarriage, was without vice, and was easy to fly. But you sat behind a Rolls Royce liquid-cooled engine (as in the Spitfire and Hurricane), the Master went quite fast, and it was fully aerobatic.

At the beginning of February I arrived at Duxford, near Cambridge to get my first glimpse of the fabulous Spitfire. The next day I flew it. I sat in the cockpit while a young Pilot Officer, with little experience, showed me the knobs. He omitted to tell me one important thing about the undercarriage operation which embarrassed me in due course, fortunately without damage.

The immediate impression that a new type of aeroplane makes remains in one's mind however many hours one flies it later. The Spitfire looked good and was good. But my first reaction was that it was bad for handling on the ground; its long straight nose, uptilted when the tail wheel was on the ground, made taxying difficult since it was not easy to see ahead. It was necessary to swing from side to side to look in front. The view at take-off was restricted in the same way until you were travelling fast enough to lift the tail; only then could you see over the nose.

Once accustomed to these minor inconveniences, they were no longer apparent, and once in the air, you felt in the first few minutes that here was the aeroplane *par excellence*. The controls were light, positive and synchronized: in fact, the aeroplane of one's dreams. It was stable; it flew hands and feet off; yet you could move it quickly and effortlessly into any attitude. You brought it in to land at 75 m.p.h. and touched down at 60–65 m.p.h. Its maximum speed was 367 m.p.h. You thus had a

---

* Douglas Bader had lost his legs in a flying accident in 1931 and had left the R.A.F. He learned to walk on artificial legs, and returned to the R.A.F. when the war broke out.

wide speed range which has not been equalled before or since.

Such was the Spitfire I. It had eight machine guns of ·303 calibre each, mounted four in each wing. The guns were spaced one close to the fuselage, two mid-wing, one further out. The eight guns were normally synchronized to 250 yards. In other words the four in each wing were sighted so that the bullets from all eight converged at that distance, in front of the Spitfire. Experienced fighter pilots used to close the pattern to 200 yards. The successful pilots succeeded because they did not open fire until they were close to the target.

The Spitfire I had a single fault which was eliminated after the Battle of Britain. The aeroplane itself was made of metal but the ailerons, instead of being covered with sheet metal, were covered with fabric. As a result they distorted from about 220 m.p.h. upwards, making the lateral control heavy and less effective with speed. This was a design fault. I asked Jeffrey Quill, the Supermarine test pilot, about it and he told me the reason. When the Spitfire was in its prototype stage it was much faster than anything there had been before. As a result, the design staff decided to play safe. In the past, some Royal Air

The superb lines of the Spitfire

Force biplane fighters had experienced aileron flutter and similar excitements through the ailerons being over-balanced. Therefore they were cautious with the Spitfire and erred, the opposite way. The non-technical pilot like myself merely noted the heaviness of the control at speed and put it down to distortion because the aileron was not covered with metal. When the aileron was modified, the Spitfire controls were quite superb.

In fairness to the design staff of Supermarine it must be said that everyone, both in the Air Ministry and elsewhere, thought that this new high-speed monoplane fighter would never be used for dog-fighting in the classic context of World War I. In fact, they were proved wrong as soon as the Hurricane or Spitfire ran into their enemy opposite numbers. When this happened, dog-fights started and the small circles which the World War I aeroplanes made at 100–120 m.p.h. merely became larger circles at 200–240 m.p.h.

I well remember some Air Ministry instructions which were sent round the fighter squadrons suggesting methods of fighter attacks against enemy bombers. Even at the time they struck me as absurd—as indeed they proved to be. Some of us held the belief, which was proved right in the event, that First World War fighter pilots like Bishop, Ball, McCudden, Mannock, and the rest knew best. They had done it. We, who had read their books, studied their methods which proved to be right. They had three basic rules: one, if you had the height you controlled the battle; two, if you came out of the sun the enemy could not see you; three, if you held your fire until you were very close you seldom missed. All sorts of other things could and did happen in combat in World War II, especially against bombers, but if you stuck to these rules your chances of survival would be reasonable.

In April 1940, I left 19 Squadron to become a Flight Commander in 222 Squadron (Spitfires) commanded by Squadron Leader Tubby Mermagen. This was also at Duxford and Tubby,

like Geoffrey Stephenson, was an exact contemporary of mine and an old friend. We used to play rugby together. Soon after joining 222, the Squadron went from Duxford to Kirton-in-Lindsay, just south of the Humber.

One early morning towards the end of May, we were ordered down to Martlesham, near Ipswich, in Suffolk. By this time the fighting had started in earnest. The Germans had smashed through the Allied defences in northern France and were sweeping towards the Channel ports. Evacuation of the British Expeditionary Force from Dunkirk had begun, and all available fighters were being sent to south-eastern airfields to cover this operation.

My first combat experience came during this phase. We were all flying around up and down the coast near Dunkirk looking for enemy aircraft which seemed also to be milling around with no particular cohesion. The sea from Dunkirk to Dover during these days of the evacuation looked like any coastal road in England on a bank holiday. It was solid with shipping. One felt one could walk across without getting one's feet wet, or that's what it looked like from the air. There were naval escort vessels, sailing dinghies, rowing-boats, paddle-steamers, indeed every floating device known in this country. They were all taking British soldiers from Dunkirk back home. The oil-tanks just inside the harbour were ablaze, and you could identify Dunkirk from the Thames estuary by this huge pall of black smoke rising straight up in a windless sky. Our ships were being bombed by enemy aeroplanes up to about half-way across the Channel and the troops on the beaches were suffering the same attention. There were also German aircraft inland strafing the remnants of the British Expeditionary Force fighting their way out to the port.

I was flying along at about 3,000 feet when an Me 109 appeared straight in front of me at about the same speed and going in the same direction. Like me, he must have been a beginner, because he stayed there while I shot him down, and I didn't get him with the first burst.

A day or two later I saw a Dornier bombing one of our ships. He was about a mile away and I rushed at him with the throttle wide open giving myself just time for a hurried burst which silenced the rear-gunner. I had to pull up quickly to avoid a collision. Thinking about it later on that evening I got the message which every fighter pilot assimilates early in his career —if he hopes for a career at all. It is this: overtake your target slowly and relax before you start shooting; you will never get him in a hurry.

That, then, was my first impression of the Spitfire in combat, although it was certainly not air-fighting in the classic style. Its outstanding quality in this respect became fully obvious to me only several months later.

There were many different versions of the basic Spitfire: for photographic reconnaissance, for dive-bombing, ground-strafing, indeed every form of air-to-air and air-to-ground requirement that could be envisaged. That lovely elliptical wing also had its ends specially chopped to make the Spitfire more manoeuvrable at low altitude for attacks on the railways and roads of occupied Europe, and later in Germany itself.

Rolls Royce fitted the Spitfire with different engines for high flying (with the elliptical wing) and for fighter combat; also with medium-altitude and low-altitude engines. Neither Spitfire nor Hurricane was built for long-range escort duties. Their flying duration under favourable circumstances was two hours. Include fifteen to twenty minutes' combat and you could count on one and a half hours. If you were in a hurry and flying with a wide throttle and high r.p.m. then the engine fairly 'gulped the gravy'. This was true of both aeroplanes in the first half of the war. When the U.S. Air Force with their Flying Fortresses arrived in England and started bombing deep into the heartland of Germany, slipper tanks carrying up to ninety gallons of fuel were fitted under the Spitfire's belly thus giving it the range to escort these daylight raids.

After the war I asked Galland, the top German fighter leader, why the German fighters did not attack the daylight Allied bomber formations as they crossed the coast over the occupied countries while both the escorting fighters and the bombers were full of fuel and highly vulnerable. The Spitfires with their outside drop tanks would have had to release them in order to fight and therefore could not have continued their escort duties. Galland, who finished the war as a General Major, Inspector-General of Fighters, replied that that was exactly what the operational pilots wanted to do. Hitler had specifically forbidden it on the grounds that it was better for the morale of the German population to see the Allied aircraft shot down over Germany. He was truly mad.

At the end of June 1940, I was made a Squadron Leader and given command of 242 (Canadian) Fighter Squadron. It was equipped with Hurricanes Mark I. The only time I had flown a Hurricane, and then just for a short time, was at Upavon five months previously. That model had had a two-bladed, fixed-pitch airscrew. Now I got to know three-bladed constant speed propellers. They were better, providing shorter take-off, faster climb.

The Hurricane was slower than the Spitfire, with a maximum speed of 335 m.p.h. against 367 m.p.h. The Hurricane also was less elegant to the eye, but then there has never been such a beautiful aeroplane as the Spitfire. For all that, like other fighters from the Hawker stable, and the result of the design genius of Sydney Camm, the Hurricane was a thoroughbred and looked it. Like the Spitfire it was immensely strong: a pilot

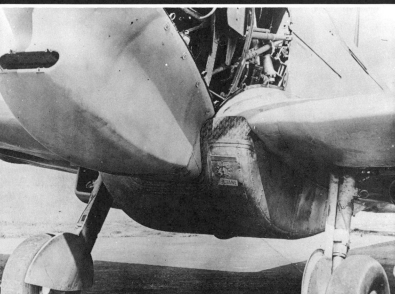

Two adaptations of the Spitfire. With clipped wings for low-level attack— workmanlike but not beautiful.

With a 90-gallon slipper-tank to increase the range

had no need to fear the danger of pulling the wings off, no matter how desperate the situation became.

When I first flew the Hurricane in June 1940, I was agreeably surprised at the compact feel of the aeroplane. It had seemed big on the ground in comparison with the Spitfire; in the air it felt nothing of the sort. You could see out of it better and the controls were perfectly harmonized. It climbed steeply and at a lower speed but required a good deal of right rudder in the climb, to counteract the engine torque. I found this a considerable nuisance on a long climb. The Spitfire had the same left-hand pull in a climb but it also had a manually operated bias in the cockpit so that the pilot could trim it out on the rudder.

As I was continually leading formations on long climbs from take-off to 20,000 feet, the maximum height at which the Hurricane I could successfully fight, I got fed-up with this. The Hawker test-pilot, Philip Lucas, was a chum, so I rang him up and complained. There were instant results (as was always the case in those days). I flew my Hurricane over to Langley where they fitted a rudder bias in hours.

Like all pilots who flew and fought in the Hurricane I, I grew to love it. It was strong, highly manoeuvrable, could turn inside the Spitfire and of course the Me 109. Best of all, it was a marvellous gun platform. The sloping nose gave you a splendid for-

ward view, while the eight guns were set in blocks of four in each wing, close to the fuselage. The aeroplane remained rock steady when you fired. Unlike the Spitfire with its lovely elliptical wing which sloped upwards to the tip, the Hurricane wing was thicker and straight. The Spitfire was less steady when the guns were firing because, I have always thought, they were spread further along the wing, and the recoil effect was noticeable.

The Hurricane was in fact a larger aeroplane than the Spitfire. Its wing-span was 40 feet, its length 31 feet 4 inches; the Spitfire's wing-span was 36 feet 10 inches and its length 29 feet 11 inches with a wing-loading of 26 lbs per square foot against the Hurricane's 24·1. This was why the Hurricane could out-turn the Spitfire. Each was powered by the same Rolls-Royce Merlin engine of 1030 horse-power. The fighting weights of the Hurricane I and the Spitfire I were almost identical—6,218 lbs. and 6,200 lbs. respectively. Later models, of course, differed widely as they were produced for all sorts of specialized combat duties. The high-flying Spitfire VI had a larger wing-span and a pressurized cockpit for operation above 30,000 feet.

My first success in a Hurricane occurred soon after I had taken over command of 242 Squadron.

One morning, at about 07.00 hours, the telephone rang in my dispersal hut on the airfield and the Operations Room Controller's voice said: 'There's a "bandit" flying up the coast towards Cromer. Can you get a section off?' In those days a section was three aeroplanes. I looked out at the airfield. There was low cloud at about 600 feet and drizzle; the visibility seemed to be about two miles. I replied: 'No. The weather is lousy. I'll have a go by myself. I shall be out of radio touch almost as soon as I leave the airfield, so I'll fly straight to the coast, turn left and go as far as Cromer. If I don't see anything, I'll come back.' I took off and discovered the cloud base was exactly 700 feet. I remember thinking what a splendid view the Hurricane had under such conditions.

At the coast the cloud base had lifted to 1,000 feet. I flew along towards Cromer wondering what on earth a German could be doing flying round the Norfolk coast below cloud.

Then I saw him 400 yards in front of me. As I closed on him I recognized the narrow fuselage and twin fins of a Dornier 17, the aeroplane nicknamed the 'flying pencil'. The enemy had not seen me. I imagine the crew did not expect to be intercepted at that height in that weather and were taking it a bit easy. Anyhow we continued flying along with my Hurricane gaining on the Dornier. At 250 yards, I had just re-set my reflector sight to 200 yards range when the enemy rear-gunner opened fire. The flashes from his machine gun were vivid. That crew had woken up!

Now, one of the defects of the German twin-engined bombers

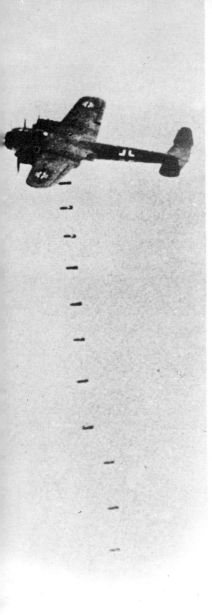

Dornier 17

of that period was their lack of effective defensive firepower. The Heinkel III, the Ju 88, the Dornier 17, and indeed the Me 110 twin-fighter (after the Ju 87 dive-bomber the easiest to shoot down) were all equally ineffective. The rear-gunner had but one (sometimes two bracketed together) machine gun which fired over the tail as defence against attack from behind. Worse still, the wretched gunner had to manhandle his gun, aim it, and fire it, in a 200 m.p.h. (or more) slipstream if his pilot had the nerve to continue flying straight and level with a fighter on his tail. I never found one pilot who did. Evasive action began with the first sign of fighter attack, unless the German bombers were flying in formation. In that case, the fire power of all rear guns was maintained until the formation was broken up. But even so, the fire power of these formations was insignificant.

I remember thinking to myself as the Dornier gunner opened fire on me: 'I've got a twelve-cylinder engine shielding me, a bullet-proof windscreen, *and* eight machine guns.' I was totally relaxed. I fired at the Dornier, observing no effect other than a steeply banked turn to the left, but he was still below the cloud. I followed him round and he straightened up after a complete 180 degrees. Then he started a shallow climb into cloud, with me in position behind him. I fired a second burst as he disappeared and continued into cloud behind him, still shooting. With blistering curses I gave him up and flew back to Coltishall where I reported failure to the Operations Room.

About fifteen minutes later the Controller telephoned to say that a Home Guard observation post had reported a Dornier crashing into the sea near Cromer at the exact time of my action. This proved a lucky start for the new C.O. of 242 Squadron. After the incident, I remember thinking how easy it had been shooting from the Hurricane. Apart from the smell of cordite in the cockpit and the noise of the guns I might have been keeping line-astern formation on the Dornier at some peace-time air display.

So by now I had flown both the Spitfire and Hurricane sufficiently to know these aeroplanes well. Indeed I was competent in the former by night as well as by day. I had fired my guns at an enemy in each of them. Before I subsequently became a prisoner of war in August 1941, I had acquired as much combat experience in the Spitfire as in the Hurricane, and had shot down the same number of enemy aircraft in one as in the other. But I have always regarded the Hurricane as the better gun platform.

Now a word about the Spitfires' and Hurricanes' main opponents.

The Luftwaffe started the war equipped with a good fighter, the Me 109, which was used throughout the war. It had two major disadvantages. First, it was not as strong as the British fighters and therefore the German pilots could not dive it as fast or for as long as we could with ours. (One of their top fighter pilots, Baltazar, had died when the wings of his Me 109 folded up on him in a dive. It happened to other German pilots too, which was bad for morale.) Secondly, the petrol tank was 'L'-shaped and fitted around the pilot's seat. This was highly vulnerable to attack, even though it was covered with armour plate.

We British fighter pilots could not know all these murky details about the 109 until afterwards. But during the Battle of Britain we soon discovered that the 109 pilots would not hold the dive and pulled out slowly. There was another significant difference between the Me 109 and the two British fighters. All three aeroplanes were powered by twelve-cylinder, liquid-cooled engines. The Rolls Royce Merlin sat upright in the Hurricane and Spitfire and was normally aspirated with a carburettor. But the Daimler-Benz in the Me 109 was inverted and used petrol injection. The normal escape method of a Me 109 pilot with a British fighter on his tail was to push the stick forward and go straight into a steep dive. With petrol injection the negative 'g' caused by this manoeuvre did not affect his engine. When the Spitfire or Hurricane pilot tried to follow, the reverse pressure impeded the flow of petrol through the carburettor of his Rolls Royce Merlin and the engine stopped instantly. The infuriating result was that by the time you came over the top and your engine had picked up, the Me 109 was thousands of feet below, if indeed you ever saw him again.

We used to discuss this problem among ourselves, to see if we could work out some method of getting at the 109 before we lost him. The method we evolved was to half-roll to start the dive thus keeping the engine going but turning our back on the Me 109; then an aileron turn to restore direction and hope to see the enemy once more. Surprisingly, this seemingly complicated idea worked quite well in practice. It was infinitely variable in application.

Once we discovered how to stay with the Me 109 at the beginning of its dive, its structural weakness became evident. The Me 109 pilot of those days would dive away at about 75 degrees (not quite vertical) but he would never hold the dive for long. On such an occasion a 109 left my Hurricane standing in the initial stage of the dive, but he started pulling out gently long before I expected and I overhauled him. My maximum airspeed on the clock, at 8,000 feet where I started to pull out, was only 320 m.p.h. and yet I was closing the gap quickly. I remember the occasion as though yesterday. The Hurricane was bigger, slower and less streamlined than the Messerschmitt or the Spitfire. It appeared impossible to catch the former in a dive, but other Hurricane pilots had similar experiences to mine.

The advantage of the Spitfire and the Hurricane in individual combat with a Me 109 was that both British aeroplanes could out-turn the German one which was why, when surprised from

Me 109—a good fighter
aeroplane. Faster than the
Hurricane and with about the
same speed and climb as the
Spitfire. But not as strong as
either

behind, the enemy's defensive manoeuvre was to push the stick forward into a dive which, in 1940, we could not follow. If we were surprised, our defence was to turn quickly and keep turning because the Me 109's radius of turn was bigger than that of the Spitfire or Hurricane and thus he could not keep you in his sights. If he was inexperienced enough to try, he would find the British fighter behind him after a couple of circuits.

Nevertheless, the Me 109 was a good fighter aeroplane. It was smaller than its British counterparts, faster than the Hurricane, and about the same in speed and climb as the Spitfire. At first it carried mixed armament consisting of two 15-mm. cannons and two machine guns. Later models from the 'F' range onwards had what some of us regarded as the best idea of all—a cannon firing through the centre of the propeller spinner. This was a brilliant innovation since, unlike having guns in the wings, the attitude of the aeroplane did not matter.

The Me 110 which appeared at Dunkirk and at Battle of Britain time was a twin-engined, two-seater fighter in which the pilot and rear-gunner sat in tandem. It took little punishment and was easy to shoot down, because it was lightly built for performance. A burst from eight machine guns destroyed it quickly. It wasn't anything like so manoeuvrable as a single-engined, single-seater fighter and relied entirely on surprise to shoot us down. It had forward-firing cannons and the rear-gunner had one (or two) machine guns which were totally ineffective except for the occasional lucky strike. When attacked by a Hurricane or Spitfire it instantly took evasive action, usually too late. Later in the war the Germans used Me 110s effectively as night-fighters.

The Focke-Wulf 190 certainly gave the British a shock. 1941 had ended with the Me 109 f and the Spitfire Vb (two cannons and four-machine guns) fighting it out on fairly even terms. Then, without warning from British intelligence sources, this startling aeroplane appeared in March 1942. A radial-engined fighter, it out-climbed and out-dived the Spitfire. Now for the first time the Germans were out-flying our pilots. Instantly Rolls and Supermarine retaliated with the Spitfire IXa which equalled the 190, followed at the end of 1942 with the IXb which outflew it in all respects. The Spitfire was unchallenged for the rest of the war, except in the last few months by the Messerschmitt 262 jet which arrived too late to make a significant contribution.

Now, the German bombers. The Ju 87 (the Stuka), a single-engined dive-bomber, was probably the easiest enemy aircraft in the war to shoot down because it dived straight and pulled up straight. This was a requirement of its special type of bombing.

The He 111 was large and slow and was also not a difficult aircraft to shoot down.

The Dornier 17 and 215 were both known as the 'flying pencil' because they had a narrow fuselage with twin fins at the end.

Me 110—easy meat; below: proof. Inset above: the best they had—the Focke-Wulf 190

Bombers. Right: Dornier 17,
normal view. Far right and
far right below: Ju 87 dive-
bombers—Stukas. Below:
He 111s—large, slow, and easy
to shoot down

The Ju 188 (inset right) was the later version of the Ju 88, which was often mistaken for the Bristol Blenheim bomber (large picture). The technical drawing of the Ju 88 (top) shows similarities to the Blenheim (bottom)

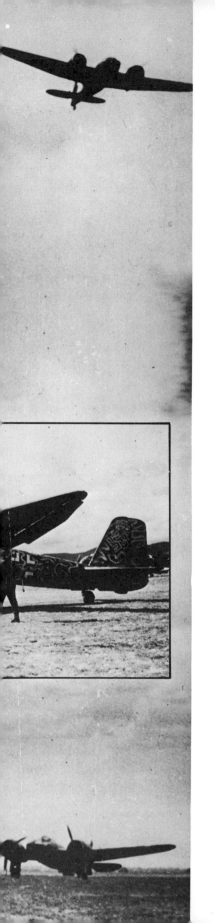

They were good-looking aeroplanes but were unable to take much punishment.

I had two personal experiences in July 1940 of shooting down two Dornier 17s. Neither seemed badly damaged when I last saw them disappearing into cloud, but even so both were later reported as crashing.

The tough German bomber was the Ju 88. It could take a great deal of punishment and still go on flying.

The problem of the Ju 88 was aggravated by the fact that at certain angles it looked identical to our Bristol Blenheim. Both were twin-engined medium bombers and both had roughly the same performance. In July 1940 my squadron, 242, shared the same airfield, Coltishall, with 66 Squadron (Spitfires) commanded by an old Cranwell chum, Rupert Leigh, a great humourist. We were frequently sent off to intercept 'enemy' aircraft which turned out to be Blenheims from bomber stations near to us, such as Horsham St Faith, a few miles away at Norwich, as well as from other airfields in Norfolk. Our personal experiences were much the same as those of other fighter squadrons.

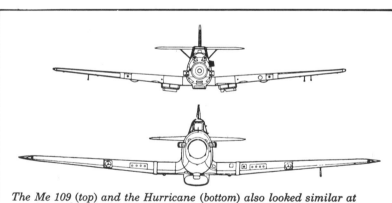

The Me 109 (top) and the Hurricane (bottom) also looked similar at certain angles. Early in the war a Spitfire squadron spotted what they thought to be four Me 109s. They attacked, but unfortunately their target was four Hurricanes—who in turn thought their attackers were Germans in captured Spitfires! The resulting melee, which took place over the Thames estuary, earned the name 'The Battle of Barking Creek'

The Blenheims got fed up with being intercepted by our fighters, so some desk-bound magician worked out that when friendly fighters approached menacingly, the Blenheim rear-gunner fired a Very pistol which contained the 'colours of the day'. These could be a variety of red and green, or two greens or two reds (no one knew what the colours of the day were supposed to be anyhow). The Germans cottoned on to this fairly quickly and they started shooting out colours of the day as well, so the result was back to square one.

One day the pilots of both squadrons at Coltishall, who were at thirty minutes' availability (i.e. could be called to immediate readiness at thirty minutes' notice), were playing rounders. The noise of an aeroplane almost overhead caused some of us to look up and then ignore it thinking 'it's only a Blenheim'— then it dropped a stick of bombs across the airfield and on one hangar. It was, of course, a Ju 88. Furiously we rushed to the telephone and asked the Operations Room what the hell they thought they were doing. Needless to say the Operations Room was not on the airfield. A few days later another 'Ju 88' appeared. Both squadrons leapt into their aeroplanes with the result that twelve Hurricanes and twelve Spitfires took to the air and chased the bomber. It was, of course, a Blenheim. Acrimonious discussions followed between the two Squadron Leaders and the Station Commander; later a better system was devised.

But to return to our own aeroplanes. The last time I flew a Spitfire in combat—or for that matter any other aeroplane in combat—was over northern France in the morning of August 1941, a Saturday, a typical summer day with scattered cloud at 4,000 feet and blue sky above.

Since March we had been operating offensive patrols over the Channel coast of Europe almost daily. From May onwards the Tangmere Wing, which I led, and other Wings in 11 Group of Fighter Command had been escorting bombers over northern France attacking military targets of which there were plenty around St Omer, Bethune, Lille, Douai and of course Cherbourg and Le Havre.

On this occasion we crossed the coast of France near Le Touquet, looking for the Me 109s from Abbeville or Wissant (behind Boulogne) with whom we usually tangled. The 109s from Merville and St Omer were further inland. As we crossed into France all four of us in the front section, 'Cocky' Dundas, 'Johnnie' Johnson, and my New Zealander number two, Jeff West, all saw them simultaneously; twelve Me 109s in similar formation to ours—three sections of four—2-3,000 feet below us, a mile or two in front, going the same way and climbing—a perfect situation for the classic attack from behind and above.

But the Tangmere wing-leader did everything wrong. I signalled 'attacking' and dived down too fast and too steeply. I was tense, and my judgement had gone for some reason which I did not recognize at the time. One never did. I behaved as I had done on my first glimpse of an enemy over the sea off Dunkirk in May 1940. I closed so fast on the 109 that I had no time to fire, and barely time to avoid cutting him in half with my Spitfire. I continued diving and levelled out at 24,000 feet. I pulled myself together and had a look round. Nothing in sight, I was alone in the sky. It was always the same. One moment the sky was full of aeroplanes, the next, it was empty. I was debating whether to carry on towards the target and hope to find the others or whether to follow my own advice to my pilots when alone, which was to get down to ground level and fly home, when I noticed a couple of miles in front at the same height three pairs of 109s. There was no doubt in my mind what to do. They had come up from St Omer or Merville and were target bound. I dropped down just below them and closed up. If they saw me and turned I would

dive vertically for a few thousand feet and then go home. No 109 could stay with a Spitfire in a dive. They did not see me. I destroyed the back one of the middle pair with a short burst from close range. As he dived away on fire I closed up on his companion in front, and was just opening fire when I saw the two 109s on my left turning towards me—I decided to go home. A few bits were falling off my 109, but I'd nearly been caught that way once before when I'd thought I just had time to finish an enemy off and got a cockpit full of bullets instead.

I then made my final mistake. The rule is as old as air-fighting: always turn towards your enemy, never turn your back on him. If you do, you lose sight of him and present him with you as a target. The two enemy on my right were still flying straight which was why I turned right towards them, intending to pass over the top of them or even behind them, and then dive away for home in the opposite direction. At this stage there was no problem. (It is perhaps worth explaining in this context that there is no danger from the proximity of an enemy fighter provided his nose is not pointing at you. His guns or cannons are fixed, forward-firing. You can fly alongside each other in complete safety.) But the bad judgement which had dogged me the whole morning finally fixed me. I banked over right-handed and collided with the second 109. If I had turned left towards the 109s coming at me, there would have been no danger, except from a lucky bullet, because we would have been looking at each other. The memory is as clear today as when it happened thirty-two years ago. I felt rather than heard a noise behind the cockpit, saw the tail of a 109 out of the corner of my eye passing behind me and then got the impression that someone was grasping the tail of my Spitfire. Down went the nose vertically; I pulled the stick back and there was nothing there.

Paul Brickhill described it exactly in *Reach for the Sky* when he wrote: 'He pulled back on the stick but it fell inertly into his stomach like a broken neck'. I looked behind and there appeared to be nothing behind the cockpit. In other words the complete back end, elevator, and fin had disappeared. Time to leave.

Force of habit made me glance at the airspeed indicator and the altimeter. The latter was unwinding fast and passing 20,000 feet; the former was stationary at 400 m.p.h. I remember thinking it had been like that since a few minutes after take-off from Tangmere. It was broken and indicating 0 which roughly corresponded with 400 m.p.h. on the inner scale. What did it matter, I was proceeding earthwards fast with the Spitfire rotating slowly about its own axis.

As always, when things like this occur, one's mind remains clear. I pulled the little rubber ball above my head which jettisoned the cockpit canopy and away it went. Immediately things became rough and noisy with the wind roaring past and around the now open cockpit. I was tightly held by my harness and I had no difficulty in moving my hands. I thought I might have difficulty in getting out of the cockpit in this attitude of the aeroplane and at this great speed. I pulled the harness pin, and it was as though I was sucked out by a large vacuum cleaner to the accompaniment of tremendous noise and buffeting. My helmet and goggles were wrenched off my head and then to my final discomfort I found myself still attached to my Spitfire, but outside it. My last coherent thought was that it really had been a lousy day. I say 'coherent' because although I was conscious and my brain working perfectly, I was being subjected to so much buffeting and noise that I found it impossible to think through it.

All I knew was that something had gone wrong and that events had taken over and I had no influence over them. I remember knowing that I still held the parachute release ring in my right hand and thinking that I'd have to pull it. It all seemed to take a long time but can have lasted only a few seconds. Then suddenly the hammering noise ceased and I felt as though I was falling upwards. I pulled the parachute release and then I was floating in the sunshine above broken white cloud. I was about 4–5,000 feet above the ground. I heard an aeroplane just after I passed through the cloud. A Me 109 flew past.

The ground below was the farm and grazing land of northern France. A man wearing a peaked sort of railway porter's cap and a blue smock, carrying on his shoulders a yoke to which were attached two buckets, was opening a gate between two grass fields. A woman with a scarf over her head was with him. As he opened the gate, he noticed me about 800 feet above and in front of him. They both remained motionless, staring. I then realized that my appearance was a bit odd. My right leg was no longer with me. It had caught somewhere in the top of the cockpit as I tried to leave my Spitfire and held me to the aeroplane; and then the leather belt which attached it to my body had broken under the strain, and the leg, the Spitfire, and I had all parted company.

But the left leg was still there; these good French peasants were watching a chap arriving in a parachute with one leg, the other missing, and with a torn trouser flapping in the breeze. I felt rather embarrassed. The last 200 feet of a parachute descent were deceptive in those days. Even after the hectic moments of the last hour, indeed perhaps because of them, I was actually enjoying this quiet drifting earthwards. It was so restful after the shattering noise which had preceded it. Then—bang—the ground leapt up at me. When I became conscious a minute or so later, two German soldiers were bending over me removing my parachute harness. They carried me to a car and took me to the hospital in St Omer. A lousy day indeed.

Enough for the time being about the aeroplanes themselves and my experiences. Before recounting their history during World War II, we should take a look at the pre-war period.

THE HURRICANE

The British public became dramatically aware of their new super-fighter, the Hurricane, when Squadron Leader J. Gillan, C.O. of 111 Squadron, took off on 10 February 1938 from Turnhouse, Edinburgh, just after five o'clock on a gloomy and wild winter dusk. As reported at the time, Gillan ascended to an altitude of 17,000 feet and flew over the clouds without the aid of oxygen. An 80 m.p.h. wind whistled him southwards at a great speed. About forty minutes later, he dipped his Hurricane into a dive, registering an air-speed of 380 m.p.h. Once below the cloud, he made out Northolt airport in the early night darkness 'startled at the realization that the ground-speed was likely to be in the region of 450 m.p.h.' The statistics for the flight were as follows: 327 miles from Turnhouse to Northolt in 48 minutes at an average ground-speed of 408·75 m.p.h.

A fighter which far outstripped anything that came before it had shown its considerable paces. And as the international situation became more menacing throughout 1938 and 1939 the British people derived increasing reassurance from these squat but effective-looking shapes snarling above them through the skies.

The Hurricane story began in 1933: only six years before the war and seven before the Battle of Britain. The Royal Air Force then was equipped with just thirteen fighter squadrons. Eight were equipped with Bristol Bulldogs, three with Hawker Furies, and two with Hawker Demons. All were biplanes, with fixed propellers and undercarriages.

Monoplanes were not unknown during the 1920s. Sydney Camm—the Hurricane's designer—had evolved one, which was never built. The idea of the Hurricane was born in August 1933, when Camm talked to government officials about the way fighter design might develop, in particular the idea of the Hawker Fury in monoplane form. At that stage, Camm could not present any drawings of his scheme, but by October 1933 he had submitted a first design to the Air Ministry. This early Fury Monoplane conception incorporated a Goshawk engine, but by January 1934 it was superseded by a Rolls Royce PV12. Further design included a retractable undercarriage.

By May 1934 the 'Interceptor Monoplane', as it was now known, was designed in detail, with loaded weight assessed at 4,600 pounds. Armament consisted of a couple of wing-mounted Browning guns and two fuselage-mounted Vickers guns.

As Nazi Germany rearmed, a weapon that was to help thwart Hitler's plans took shape. A one-tenth scale model of the Hurricane was constructed in June 1934 and like so many other inventions before and since, it went to Teddington for trials at the National Physical Laboratory. The vital basic aerodynamic qualities were confirmed to be in order by August in a series of wind-tunnel tests providing the equivalent of speeds up to 350 m.p.h. A Government specification emerged at the end of August. It stipulated a single-seat interceptor fighter with a top speed of 320 m.p.h. in level flight at 15,000 feet.

Though all concerned had moved fast, time was vital. In the high summer of 1940 the Hurricane would provide the major part of the thin blue line against the German Luftwaffe.

By December 1934 a wooden mock-up of the F36/34 single-seat fighter high-speed monoplane was in existence. The next significant date was 21 February 1935, when the Air Ministry received its initial performance details. The specification had been met. The monoplane could reach a top speed of 330 m.p.h. in level flight at 15,000 feet, with a flying weight calculated at 4,480 pounds. The altitude provision was for a 32,500 feet service ceiling and 34,800 feet absolute maximum. The landing speed: just over 70 m.p.h. At this stage, further investigation was to be undertaken into the possibility of providing metal stressed-skin wings and also stepping up the armament. It was to be wartime before production aircraft actually incorporated the metal wing.

In August 1935 K5083, the first prototype, was underway, with a new PV12 Merlin engine. The increase to eight guns meant that the flying weight rose to 5,200 pounds. Hawkers had an assembly shed at Brooklands racing car track in Surrey. Here the prototype pieces were taken on 23 October 1935 and assembled.

Past and future. Sydney Camm (left), designer of the Hurricane, in front of an antiquated Hawker Cygnet. Bulman, Hawker's chief test pilot, stands on the right

Opposite: First World War
Fighter aircraft

Far left, from the top: S.E.5a,
De Havilland 2, S.P.A.D.7

Left, from the top: Fokker E1,
Fokker Triplane, Albatross D.3

Bottom: Major W. G. Barker
and Sopwith Camel

British Fighters of 1930s

Top: Hawker Demon

Centre: Hawker Fury

Bottom: Bristol Bulldog

The necessary ground tests were carried out: undercarriage retraction, engine running, taxi trials. In aircraft design no one can ever be quite sure how the actual centre of gravity will compare with the calculations, but it turned out that Sydney Camm's had been accurate to within half an inch.

On 6 November 1935, Flight Lieutenant P. W. S. Bulman, chief test pilot of Hawkers at the time, closed the cockpit of the prototype—a closed cockpit was itself an invention, previous fighters being equipped with open ones. The small silver monoplane took off for the first flight, climbing off a grass strip that was surrounded by the banked curves of the car track. No one in Britain realized then the significance of this date: the first flight of the Hurricane.

All went well on the early tests, and on 7 February 1936 Bulman was able to recommend the fighter as being ready for Royal Air Force evaluation: three months and one day after its maiden flight, a tribute to Sydney Camm's design. The two other pilots involved in the early flight programme were Philip Lucas, who flew some of the experimental work, and John Hindmarsh, who later conducted the firm's production flight

trials. This first prototype went to the R.A.F. Experimental Establishment, Martlesham Heath, Suffolk.

To many men like Winston Churchill, it seemed that time was getting desperately short, so it was as well that by the mid-1930s decisions were being taken more quickly. On 3 June 1936, Hawkers accepted a contract to construct 600 aircraft. Not a day was wasted, and within a week they had issued fuselage manufacturing drawings. Soon after this the Hurricane received official approval from the Air Ministry. Never before had such a sizeable order been given in peace time. Indeed it might be said that this order, rather than the Battle of Britain itself, was the turning-point in history.

In the course of production the firm had to provide for a number of modifications. As a result of rigorous tests by the R.A.F. of the original prototype, several snags had, not surprisingly, appeared. During these 1937 flights simulating high-speed combat duties, canopies were actually lost on five occasions. This trouble was cured by March 1938. Hitler's shadow was long over Europe.

The first production model, now with a Merlin II engine, made its maiden flight on 12 October 1937. Seven weeks later, seven were in the air. Production was increasing to the rate of thirty a month. The Merlin II engine change had put the overall production programme back. This scheme had envisaged 500 Hurricanes and 300 Spitfires in service by March 1939.

The first four Hurricanes for the Royal Air Force reached 111 Squadron at Northolt during December and a dozen more came in January and February 1938. By the spring of 1938, Kenley was the second station to see Hurricanes, when 3 Squadron got its quota of eighteen. (The strength of a squadron in the air was twelve, its total strength eighteen. The six extra aircraft were known as 'IR' or Immediate Reserve: in other words these were the aeroplanes held by the squadron as instant replacements for unserviceable aircraft. When production increased, the IR numbered nine, giving a total squadron strength of twenty-one.)

By September 1938—the time of the Munich Crisis—five R.A.F. squadrons had received Hurricane fighters. Deliveries of the Spitfire were only just starting. Perhaps it was as well for our future that the war did not break out then, instead of 1939— from the point of view of Britain's air power, the extra respite given by Chamberlain's appeasement of Hitler at Munich was vital. The intervening year enabled the Royal Air Force to double the Fighter Command strength. From the total of nearly 500 Hurricanes actually delivered to squadrons and to the reserve, about three-quarters had been built in that vital year. When war started on 3 September 1939, eighteen squadrons of R.A.F. Fighter Command were equipped with Hurricanes.

3 BIRTH OF THE SPITFIRE
From seaplane to super-fighter

The Spitfire was descended from a famous 'dynasty' of seaplanes, competitors in the Schneider Trophy, the international contest whose award went to the aeroplane with the fastest average speed over a set course. Any country winning three times in a row, would keep the trophy.

The debut of the Spitfire's direct ancestor was inauspicious. R. J. Mitchell, Supermarine's designer, had invented for the 1926 competition the S.4, a monoplane seaplane, which quickly captured the world speed record at 226·75 m.p.h. Hopes were high for the trophy but the S.4 crashed before the contest took place. By a coincidence, this was also the very year that Camm had designed his first monoplane: the one that was never built.

The Trophy was now the focus of intense international interest and considerable national prestige was attached to it. But the costs of preparing for it were well beyond the resources of a commercial company. The result was that the British Government decided to finance Britain's 1927 effort. And so in September 1927, Royal Air Force personnel formed the British Schneider Trophy team. This time the contest was to be held at Venice. The British set out with three S.5 seaplanes, developed from the S.4. Two of these were the only competitors to finish the course—and win the Trophy for Britain at 281·656 and 273·47 m.p.h. respectively.

The next Schneider Trophy year was 1929. By that time Vickers (Aviation) Ltd., had taken over R. J. Mitchell's original firm of Supermarine—and he went with it. With the endorsement of the Air Ministry for the Schneider Trophy, the S.6 went into design and production. These early seaplanes certainly had an ephemeral life, being born, flying and dying often in a matter of months.

Mitchell made a change to Rolls Royce engines for his new project, giving the famous makers only six months for the job. This S.6 design followed the lines of the S.5, but with the new engine.

The venue for this eleventh Schneider Trophy event was Spithead, off the Hampshire coast, on 7 September 1929. The British entry looked like being two S.6 models and a couple of Gloster VI seaplanes. Both the Gloster monoplane designs with Napier engines had to be withdrawn due to development trouble. So the two S.6s by R. J. Mitchell faced the only foreign competition: the redoubtable Macchi seaplanes from Italy.

The day before the race a dramatic snag occurred. After all the workmen had left for the day, a Rolls Royce engineer discovered that as a result of a seized piston, the cylinder had been scored. A new block had to be fitted. The local Southampton police traced the men, recalled them to the workshops, and actually gave them lifts to get there. By working all through the night, the job was done and the S.6 prepared for flight by 10.30—shortly before the race.

'First photograph of Great Britain's secret racing marvel of the air' was the contemporary caption to this picture of the *Supermarine S5, winner of the Schneider Trophy 1927*

Overleaf, top: the combination that was the Spitfire. R. J. Mitchell (left) and Henry Royce of Rolls Royce. Just as the design genius of Camm produced the Hurricane, so the brilliance of R. J. Mitchell produced the Spitfire. The former survived the war; the latter died from an incurable disease—still a young man, but with his mission completed

Overleaf, left to right: Supermarine S5; Supermarine S6b—outright winner of Schneider Trophy; the Vickers Supermarine F7/30—design link between S6b and Spitfire

43

The British pilot in the race was Flight Lieutenant H. R. D. Waghorn. When he was approaching, as he thought, the last of his seven circuits of fifty kilometres each, his engine failed. It gave out entirely near Cowes and so he alighted on the water off Old Castle Point, some miles from the finish. In fact he had miscounted the number of circuits—his last was his eighth. He had already won the Trophy at an average speed of 328·63 m.p.h. The other S.6 had suffered a navigational mishap earlier on. (A short while afterwards, Squadron Leader A. H. Orlebar, also in an S.6, raised the world's speed record twice—to 336·3 m.p.h. and again to 357·7 m.p.h.)

So Britain had won the Schneider Trophy twice. A third victory and it would be hers permanently. But in the bleak economic climate of 1931, the British Government refused further support. A private sponsor in the person of Lady Houston

stepped in, offering £100,000 for the purpose. Mitchell had no time to start on something entirely fresh, so he improved the S.6 into the S.6B.

This time the British had no competitors. The entries prepared by the Italians and French literally could not get off the water, and the Americans had opted out of the competition four or five years earlier. So the British were the only starters.

They needed but to complete the course to gain the Schneider Trophy outright, and this they did.

On 13 September 1931 thousands of people lined the coast and thronged the piers at Southsea, Gosport, and elsewhere. Flight Lieutenant J. W. Boothman completed the course at an average speed of 340·08 m.p.h.

On the same day, Flight Lieutenant Stainforth set up a new world speed record of 379·05 m.p.h. On 29 September he increased it to 407·05 m.p.h.

No more Schneider Trophy contests were to take place—and the Royal Air Force disbanded its High Speed Flight which had been formed especially for the project. Fortunately the experience of the Schneider Trophy was not lost. Mitchell and his staff

Winners of Schneider Troph

Date	Country
1913	FRANCE
1914	BRITAIN
1915–18	(No Contest)
1919	(Contest annulled
1920	ITALY
1921	ITALY
1922	BRITAIN
1923	U.S.A.
1924	(No contest)
1925	U.S.A.
1926	ITALY
1927	BRITAIN
1928	(No Contest)
1929	BRITAIN
1930	(No Contest)
1931	BRITAIN

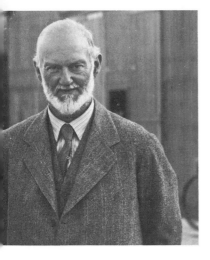

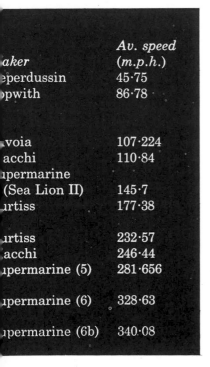

	Av. speed
...aker	(m.p.h.)
...eperdussin	45·75
...opwith	86·78
...voia	107·224
...acchi	110·84
...ipermarine (Sea Lion II)	145·7
...irtiss	177·38
...irtiss	232·57
...acchi	246·44
...ipermarine (5)	281·656
...ipermarine (6)	328·63
...ipermarine (6b)	340·08

felt that their work could be best channelled into the development of a high-speed monoplane land fighter. As soon as the Air Ministry announced its specification for a day-and-night-fighter monoplane with four guns, Mitchell urged his firm to tender.

Mitchell's offering, the Supermarine F7/30, did not meet with government approval. What it did was to act as an indispensable link design between the S.6B and the Spitfire.

In any case, a new official specification was out for an eight-gun monoplane fighter. The projected machine-gun power had been doubled, and at the same time the government decided that the gun most likely to meet the needs of the new fighter was the American Browning.

Supermarine's restyled the F7/30 to cope with this new specification.

On 5 March 1936, just four months almost to the day after the first flight of the Hurricane, the Spitfire prototype was flown from Eastleigh airfield by Captain J. 'Mutt' Summers, chief test pilot of the Vickers group. An onlooker described the new machine as 'a highly polished silvery monoplane that looked almost ridiculously small, with a seemingly enormous wooden propeller'. The machine took off, the undercarriage went up, and in a minute the Spitfire became a dot in the Hampshire sky. So far so good. Then Mitchell had to turn the prototype into the production model, complete with eight-gun armament.

In 1936 the British public had not heard of either of these two magic names, Spitfire and Hurricane. The Spitfire appeared for the first time in public on Saturday 27 June 1936 at the famous pre-war R.A.F. Hendon Display. The prototype Hurricane flew on the same day, skimming the crowd just before the Spitfire. It was the first time the two had flown in proximity. Not the last!

With his eye on the Air Ministry's production scheme promulgated in 1936, Squadron Leader Ralph Sorley, R.A.F. officer responsible for the development of the Spitfire, wanted Spitfire production started early in 1936. In the event, the order was placed only four months after the first flight of the prototype. The agreement was dated 3 July 1936. The contract was for

310 Spitfires to fulfil the 1936 plan for 500 Hurricanes and 300 Spitfires in service by March 1939.

Before the war this sort of mass production represented a vast task to an aviation manufacturer. The stressed-skin construction called for tooling that was both expensive and time-consuming. Tragically, R. J. Mitchell died on 11 June 1937 when only forty-two years old and before he could see the first Spitfire off the production line. The first Spitfire was in fact flight tested in May 1938. That autumn of 1938, Vickers (Aviation) and the Supermarine Aviation Works (Vickers) both became part of Vickers-Armstrong.

In 1938, at the time of Munich, Fighter Command of the Royal Air Force had twenty-nine fighter squadrons. Of these only five had modern equipment—i.e. Hurricanes. Pilots of the other twenty-four squadrons were flying obsolete biplanes with fixed undercarriages, insignificant fire-power, and maximum level speeds of around 220 m.p.h. *This was one year before the beginning of World War II.*

The first Spitfire to go into the Royal Air Force reached 19 Squadron at Duxford on 4 August 1938. This had a two-bladed wooden propeller and no armour behind the seat for the pilot's protection. The rate of arrival after this first Spitfire was one a week. 19 and 66 Squadrons, both at Duxford, were the first two to be equipped with Spitfires during the next weeks. On March 8 1939, it was officially announced that the Spitfire maximum level speed was 362 m.p.h. at 18,500 feet and that its rate of climb was around 2,000 feet per minute. At last we had a fighter comparable to any in the world. The two squadrons at Duxford were followed by 41 Squadron at Catterick in Yorkshire, then 74 and 54 Squadrons both stationed at Hornchurch in Essex.

In July 1939 a two-pitch airscrew (coarse and fine) was fitted to the Spitfire which increased its top speed to 367 m.p.h. In August—less than four weeks before the outbreak of World War II—these airscrews were being fitted to all production Spitfires.

The public first saw a Spitfire in R.A.F. colours on Empire Air Day, 20 May 1939. The pilot belly-landed during the Duxford display and afterwards was fined £5 by the Air Ministry.

It was not unusual in those early days for pilots to forget to lower the undercarriage before landing. After all they had never had to do so before throughout their flying career! The small fine, which was soon discontinued, was a typical bureaucratic method of reprisal. The real answer was cockpit routine, or discipline, which newer pilots were taught from the beginning.

On 3 September, 1939, there were some 400 Spitfires already in service, and over 2,000 on order. A very different state of affairs from a year earlier. But Britain was still short of fighters, and, worse still, of pilots to fly them.

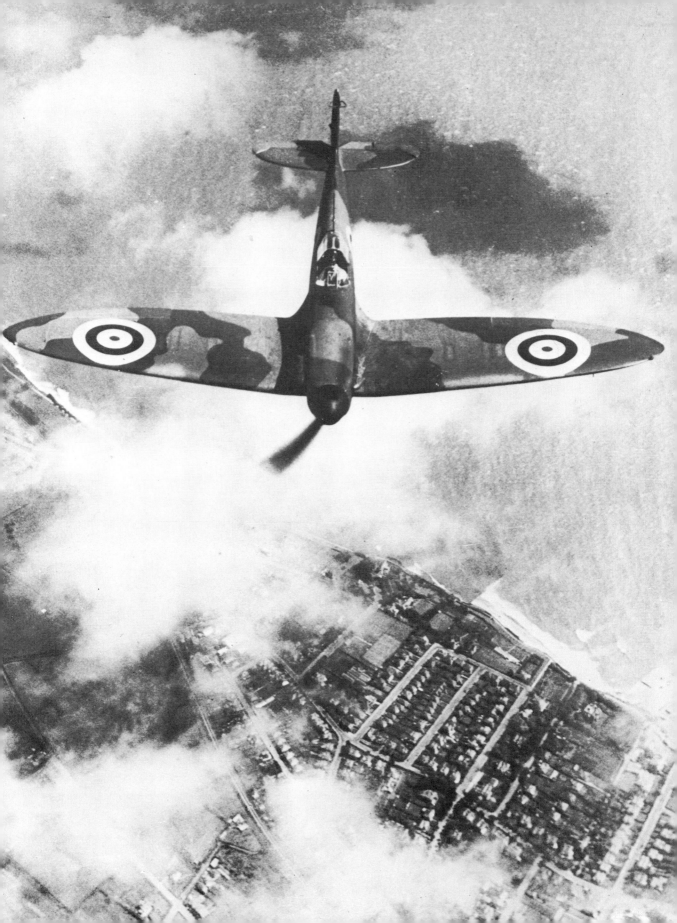

4 THE BATTLE OF FRANCE
First blood

Little happened during the first winter of the war. The period was known as the 'phoney war'. In retrospect it was an odd phrase because, quite obviously, the Germans were not going to start an offensive on the Western Front during the winter. At any rate it was a good opportunity for us British to try to plug the gaps in our defences caused by chicanery, stupidity, dishonesty, and the criminal negligence of our politicians since the late 1920s.

The British Expeditionary Force together with the Advance Air Striking Force (A.A.S.F.) had gone to France as soon as the Germans had invaded Poland in September 1939. The British Army crossed the Channel singing 'We'll hang out our washing on the Siegfried Line' (the German defence system opposite the ill-fated French Maginot Line). Our soldiers were equipped with rifles, machine guns, and waterproof plastic bags in which they could keep dry their letters from home! The A.A.S.F. was more fortunate; at least the fighter squadrons were equipped with Hurricanes. The remainder of the R.A.F. in France was not so lucky, having slow, unwieldly, highly vulnerable aeroplanes like Fairey Battles, a two-seater, single-engined type, virtually defenceless against a fighter.

When war broke out, Air Chief Marshal Sir Hugh Dowding was Commander-in-Chief of R.A.F. Fighter Command. He was the most senior officer in the Royal Air Force. He had been due to retire in 1938, but had been asked to continue as C.-in-C. Fighter Command. He was a man of utter integrity, dedicated to the service of his country. Devoid of personal ambition, he stated what he believed, indifferent to the antagonisms of senior civil servants or politicians. He laid the foundations for victory in the Battle of Britain in 1940.

Several years earlier he had recognized the great potential of radar and had persuaded parsimonious Whitehall officials of the necessity to erect early-warning radar stations on Britain's south-east coastline. In its infancy, radar was known as R.D.F. —radio direction finding—and it gave R.A.F. controllers on the ground advance information of enemy aircraft approaching our shores from fifty miles away, which with the cruising speeds of those days (180–200 m.p.h.) meant fifteen to twenty minutes' warning.

There are many stories of Dowding and his battles with Whitehall and they are all to his credit. They do not, unfortunately form part of this book. Let it suffice to say that without his keen intellect, his grasp of the essential, and his forthright method of expression, Fighter Command might not have been fit to resist the German air attacks in the high summer of 1940. First and foremost Dowding insisted that the British air defences should not be depleted in favour of overseas commitments. In other words, despite France asking for a minimum of ten fighter squadrons to support her on the Continent, it was agreed that only four Hurricane squadrons should cross the Channel at first. He was determined to keep all the Spitfires based in Britain.

The four Hurricane Squadrons chosen were 85 and 87 as part of the Air Component, with 1 and 73 as part of the Allied Air Striking Force; 607 and 615, both Auxiliary squadrons, joined the Air Component later. The Hurricane strength eventually did expand to the ten squadrons originally demanded by the French.

1 Squadron reached Vassincourt on 15 September and 73 Squadron had already arrived at Caen five days earlier. The former recorded its first air victories in October and the latter a few days afterwards in early November. 73 Squadron's initial success was credited to Flying Officer E. J. Kain—later known as 'Cobber' Kain. He shot down a Dornier 17 and then later in the month another one at the then record height for air combat of 27,000 feet. This young New Zealander, the first 'ace' of the war, continued to score successes steadily. Tragically and wastefully he died in June 1940 doing a victory roll over his home airfield. A 'victory roll' was a phrase invented by the Press to describe a fighter pilot returning from a successful sortie, rolling his aeroplane over his home aerodrome before landing to let those on the ground know that he'd shot down an enemy. In fact it was rarely done because few pilots were stupid enough to risk placing the added strain of an aerobatic manoeuvre on a Hurricane or Spitfire which might have been damaged in combat. In fact Cobber Kain's death was caused by a misjudgement when leaving his airfield in France to fly home to England on leave and not on returning from combat. When I was a cadet at the Royal Air Force College, Cranwell, in 1928, there was a picture on the wall of the flight office; it showed a World War I British fighter at the top of a loop with one of the wings breaking off; the caption was: 'The last loop'. I never forgot it.

No Spitfires had been sent to France. The first to encounter the Luftwaffe were from two squadrons of the Royal Auxiliary Air Force, 602 and 603, based at Turnhouse (Edinburgh).

On 16 October a lone enemy Ju 88 ventured over the Firth of Forth and was shot down at 14.45 by a section of 603 Squadron led by Squadron Leader E. H. Stevens. It crashed into the sea and three of the four Germans survived. At 15.00 on the same day a second Ju 88 was shot down by a section of 602 Squadron. Two of its crew members were rescued from the sea. Squadron Leader Stevens therefore won by a short head the honour of being the first pilot in Fighter Command to destroy an enemy aircraft over home territory.

Then on 28 October Spitfires from each squadron went into action again. Their respective sections pounced on a lone Heinkel 111. Although two out of four of the German crew were killed, the pilot managed to land it amid the Lammermuir Hills—the first enemy to crash on British soil since 1918.

The great man himself—Air Chief Marshal Sir Hugh Dowding, Commander-in-Chief, Fighter Command

On 20 November three Spitfires from the famous 74 (Tiger) Squadron found an He 111 high off Southend. They shot it up but only the following day was their success confirmed when two of the crew of the Heinkel were found in a dinghy off the Essex coast. Thus in the first few weeks of the war one or two pilots and aircrew of the much vaunted Luftwaffe found themselves intercepted and destroyed by Spitfires which were to prove their scourge for the rest of the war.

On the whole, the period up to May 1940 was a quiet one. But in that month the Allied armies felt the full force of the Blitzkrieg. On 10 May 1940 the storm broke. The enemy Panzers trampled the defences of Holland and Belgium, while Luftwaffe bombs rained down on seventy airfields in France and the Low Countries.

The Hurricane squadrons went into immediate action, the six squadrons augmented by three more—3, 79 and 504. On 13 May 1940 Dowding sent out thirty-two more Hurricanes plus pilots, before he decided to stop. By then the proportions of our aircraft and pilot strengths overseas were forty per cent of regular fighter pilots and one-third of fighter aircraft.

The losses in the first week of that mid-May offensive amounted to twenty-two Hurricanes in actual combat and fifteen damaged on airfields—but they destroyed nearly double that total figure of German aircraft. By 17 May, exactly a week after the first attack, only three squadrons could be said to be near operational strength. On 21 May, the order was issued for all the pilots and Hurricanes to fly back to bases in England. Events, however, were to defer this return.

Meanwhile in Britain, Spitfires had been increasingly active since the German invasion of the Low Countries. Two Spitfire squadrons had tasks outside the normal range of their duties. 74 Squadron had provided air cover for a destroyer bringing the Dutch Royal Family from Holland to England. And 92 Squadron detailed four of its Spitfires as fighter escort to a Flamingo aircraft carrying Mr Churchill to France on 16 May, with his message to the French that they could expect no further air fighter forces to be spared from Britain.

From 23 May, Spitfires found themselves ranged against the Luftwaffe in mass encounters. Flying from Hornchurch, 92 Squadron ran into half a dozen Me 109s in the Dunkirk/Calais region, eliminating all six for the destruction of one Spitfire. Later the same day and still in the same area the squadron got tied up with a large force of 110s. The score—seventeen to three in our favour.

By now the order had been given for both Hurricanes and Spitfires based in Britain to assist in stopping the Luftwaffe from decimating the British Expeditionary Force. The great Dunkirk evacuation started on 26 May. The R.A.F. was extremely active throughout this famous withdrawal but such is the nature of aerial combat that the skirmishes seldom occurred in sight of the actual evacuation beaches. Typical of the successes: 19 Squadron (Spitfires) destroyed six Ju 87s and six Me 109s.

In the thick of it at this time was 'Al' Deere—destined to be shot down seven times and survive the war with a magnificent record. Like most others, this great fighter pilot from New Zealand had sat in a Spitfire for the first time earlier in 1940 and said: 'A Spitfire is the most beautiful and easy aircraft to fly and has no tricks or peculiarities normally attributable to high-speed fighters'.

He was shot down twice in two days at Dunkirk. Typically, he said the first time gave him 'little trouble'. The second must be recorded.

During a patrol over the evacuation beaches his Spitfire was hit in the glycol tank. This was always fatal to the aeroplane since the coolant drained and the engine overheated and seized in a matter of seconds rather than minutes. Al crash-landed his Spitfire on the beach knocking himself out in the process. When he came round a minute or two later, he was aware of the engine smoking menacingly. Urgently, he ripped off his straps, leapt out of the cockpit, and sat down on the beach. At that moment he could only curse his bad luck rather than appreciate his good luck at being alive. He had commanded his flight barely one hour before being clobbered.

During the Dunkirk period three fighter squadrons were operating from Biggin Hill: 213 and 242 were detailed to try and cover the Allied Expeditionary Force as it began its evacuation

Dunkirk evacuation, May/June 1940

German fighters
alongside the cliffs of
Dieppe

from France, while the third, squadron 229, was kept in the defensive role. 242 was the great Hurricane squadron I commanded soon afterwards.

On 28 May, 213 Squadron of Hurricanes had their first taste of Dunkirk as they flew straight into a scene of Junkers and Heinkels on the verge of bombing British troops far below on and off the beaches. Messerschmitts were acting as escorts. The squadron tore into the enemy so effectively as to knock down seven of them for the loss of a single Hurricane pilot. From that moment on, both 213 and 242 became airborne four, five, even six times a day. In these hectic hours, the two squadrons totalled twenty-six Dunkirk victories at a cost of nine Hurricanes and five pilots.

The whole of 242 Squadron successes in this phase could be epitomized by the young, dedicated Canadian from Calgary, Willie McKnight. He shot down a Me 109 over Dunkirk on that very first day, followed by a couple more plus a Dornier 17 on 29 May. Two days later, he got two Me 110s and on 1 June a pair of Junkers 87s with two more probables. Later that year he brought his personal score to something like sixteen and a half by the end of the Battle of Britain. Then in January 1941, he flew on one of the original low-level intruder missions aimed against the Germans in France. Six Me 109s attacked McKnight and he was killed.

Some years after the war I visited Calgary which was the home town of William McKnight. In a speech at a Chamber of Commerce lunch, I suggested to the Mayor and some of the senior citizens that they should name some of their streets—and indeed the new Calgary Airport then being built—after some of the Canadian pilots of World War II. I visited Calgary many times in the 1950s and 60s and there is now a new road leading to the airport which is called McKnight Boulevard. Later I unveiled a commemorative plaque to Willie McKnight in the passenger hall of Calgary airport. A fine tribute to a great Canadian pilot who died at the age of twenty-one.

The Hurricane squadrons still in France fought furiously as well. On 27 May there occurred what is believed to be one of the most remarkable short air battles involving Hurricanes. 501 Squadron was one of the last remaining in France. The squadron was based at Anglure, fifty miles east of Paris, and operating from a forward strip at Boos, five miles south of Rouen. Thirteen Hurricanes were airborne at 13.45 hours, led by Flying Officer E. Holden, briefed to patrol the area Abancourt-Blangy (thirty miles north-east of Rouen). They intercepted twenty-four Heinkel 111Ks escorted by twenty Me 110s. It was a massacre. Eleven Heinkels were definitely destroyed, and others damaged. The Hurricanes themselves suffered hardly any damage in this encounter, all pilots returning safely.

About one-third of the 229 R.A.F. aircraft lost throughout the

Hurricanes in line astern over France, 1940

whole Dunkirk period were Spitfires—a fair measure of the part played by the aeroplanes. The final operation by Spitfires in this phase was on 12 June when they again escorted a Flamingo bearing Mr Churchill on his last flight to and from France.

Three days later, on 15 June, almost all the Hurricanes remaining on French soil had to be destroyed.

The statistics made grim reading: of 261 Hurricanes, 75 had been shot down or destroyed on the ground as a result of enemy activity; 120 were unserviceable or lacked the fuel to fly home and so were burnt on French airfields; 66 were flown home to England with the chance to fly and fight again. In ten days, the R.A.F. had lost Hurricanes equivalent to about a quarter of its overall fighter strength. (Other figures quoted are 66 Hurricanes lost by A.A.S.F. and 219 machines of Fighter Command).

Aircraft losses, though serious, could be replaced. Pilots were a different matter. A number of experienced pilots had been killed, wounded or taken prisoner. Replacement was a real anxiety.

Britain now stood alone. The country, and in particular the Royal Air Force, awaited the air attack which was bound to be launched by the Luftwaffe as the prelude to the attempted invasion. It was at this time that the photographic reconnaissance version of the Spitfire came into its own. We needed to know what was happening across the Channel. There were four PRU Spitfires in the Royal Air Force as early as February 1940. These were under the control of Fighter Command. In June they were transferred to Coastal Command. These were unarmed high-flying aeroplanes carrying only cameras. They reckoned to fly above fighter or flack intervention. Throughout the war, but especially at this most dangerous period in our history, they did valuable work and their pilots in my view were men of great courage. It was a lonely job.

These PRU Spitfires were not always beyond enemy interception as Pilot Officer W. B. Parker discovered when he was intercepted by two Me 109s over Kent and his Spitfire was shot to bits. He bailed out at 29,000 feet, immediately losing consciousness through lack of oxygen. At about 12,000 feet he recovered and found his flying-suit was on fire. Not keen on aerial cremation, he undid his parachute harness to remove the parachute. At that moment his shoulder-straps, which were charred, broke and Parker found himself upside down but still connected to his parachute by the lower harness. In this attitude some of his clothes just fell away from him and the fire began to die down. He landed in a Kentish field—his main damage a broken arm.

Now, the stage was set for the Battle of Britain. It had been estimated that fifty-two fighter squadrons were the minimum required to defend our island. By the fall of France, in the latter half of June, the count was thirty-six the majority of which were equipped with Hurricanes.

Spitfire v Messerschmitt– a first encounter by 'Al' Deere

Me 109s in formation

I thought a fitting postscript to this chapter would be an account of the air-fighting over Dunkirk. I thus asked 'Al' Deere to write down some of his experiences. Here they are:

I was one of the fortunate few who when war broke out was a fully trained fighter pilot, flying Spitfires in 54 Squadron of which I had been a member since August 1938. Based at Hornchurch in Essex, with its sister squadrons 65 and 74, the Squadron had as its primary task the defence of the eastern approaches to London.

In the event, the squadron's first operational sorties were concerned neither with its primary task nor were they flown over home territory, but over Dunkirk, in a fourteen-day sustained effort to afford air cover for the evacuating British forces.

In that short period of time the Squadron lost one-third of its pilot strength, including both flight commanders. A heavy blow, yes, but one from which much experience was gained and many lessons learned, and these were to prove invaluable in the major battle ahead.

For my part, I had proved to my satisfaction, if not to my sceptical superiors, that in the Spitfire Ia we had a fighter which was superior overall to its immediate counterpart the Messerschmitt 109e. I had good reason to know because in a prolonged dog-fight, of the First World War type, I had tested the Spitfire against the Messerschmitt and the former proved that, except in the initial part of a dive, it could outfly the German machine.

The encounter which led to this assessment took place on the morning of 23 May in the cloud-specked skies above Calais, a focal point in the B.E.F. withdrawal. That morning, the C.O. of 74 Squadron had been forced through engine trouble to land on Calais airfield, and it had been decided to send a two-seater trainer to bring him back. 'Prof.' Leathart, C.O. 54 Squadron, was to fly the Miles Master, and myself with Johnnie Allen as number two, were to provide the escort.

On arrival over Calais airfield, I ordered Johnnie (Red 2) to patrol above the broken cloud while I circled the airfield; he was to rejoin when the Master was again safely airborne with the two C.O.s on board. I had barely completed a circuit and the Master had just landed when I was startled into awareness by Johnnie screaming over the R/T, 'Al, Red One, there's a gaggle of 109s coming in fast from the east, what'll I do?'

I shot upright in my seat—or as near upright as my seat harness would allow—and my stomach seemed at the same time to do a

Deere receives DFC *from King (Dowding, left)*

somersault. Excitedly, I replied, 'Keep them occupied, Red 2, I must stay here to see Red Leader airborne safely.' 'OK, Red 1, I'll do my best', came the reply, this time in a relatively calm voice.

At that precise moment two things happened; a Me 109 darted from the clouds to the east of the airfield and the Master commenced its take-off run from the airfield. Simultaneously with the Master becoming airborne the Me 109 opened fire, his guns spitting red tracer towards the gradually accelerating and now violently turning trainer. But it was unfortunate for the German that when first I saw him I was flying across his line of approach enabling me to turn quickly onto his tail and, though out of range, I opened fire immediately. This warning salvo had the desired effect for it caused him to bank away from the Master, and turning right towards the coast he manoeuvred to see what intruder had upset his plans. Unfortunately for him but to my great good luck, his turn brought me well inside his orbit and in so doing it placed me in an ideal firing position. He realized this and right away he commenced to climb for cloud cover and, perhaps, the support of his companions above. I knew they were above because as I closed in to range, Johnnie's voice, now very breathless, crackled in my earphones 'Red 1, can you help? I'm surrounded.'

I couldn't answer at once; the 109 was now nicely aligned in my reflector sight and my eight Brownings were pouring hot lead into his grey belly. And to some effect. With smoke pouring from his engine the German fighter spun into an uncontrolled dive and plummeted into the sea. Quickly I swung back to look for the Master but it was nowhere to be seen. It was, I thought, either shot down or safely on its way, and since it carried no R/T there was no way of knowing. I must now help Johnnie.

'Coming up Red 2. Are you O.K.?' There was no response, and as it happened no time for further R/T calls for as I popped through the broken cumulus I saw two Me 109s crossing above and heading inland. I gave chase. Obviously I too had been spotted, for they immediately went into a steep left-hand turn which I had no difficulty in holding, but they had the advantage of height. Nevertheless, I was more favourably placed below and inside the turn, and whereas when the manoeuvre first started I was definitely the hunted, I soon became the hunter. With throttle wide open I pulled my willing Spitfire curving upwards into an ideal position from which to open fire. At the first burst, which produced no apparent hits, the number two peeled away from his leader and dived downwards and inland seemingly for home leaving his leader to fight his own battle. Thus the stage was set for the first sustained dog-fight between a Spitfire and a Messerschmitt, and the puffy-white clouds drifting above the patterned French countryside were the only witnesses to this historic encounter. In fact this encounter at 10.35 hours was the first recorded combat between the two aircraft.

At first the 109 pilot continued in his turn but he soon realized that not only was I closing the range but I was able to hold the vital inside position. Quickly he rolled into a reverse turn and at the same time he pulled up into a steep climb. Momentarily, I lost distance, but as the climb continued I closed steadily causing him to adopt a new tactic, and one which really caught me by surprise. One moment I was watching his tail and the next I was presented with a full view of his pale-blue underbelly, as pushing his stick abruptly forward he went from a steep climb into a steep dive. Involuntarily, I pushed hard forward on the control column at which the engine cut dead as the carburettor, momentarily starved of petrol under the force of negative 'g', failed to function. Quickly, I rolled onto my back, and pulling hard back gained speed and engine power before again rolling out into the chase. In a matter of seconds the 109 had gained valuable distance, putting it well out of firing range. Slowly, but obviously noticeably to the German pilot, I again closed the range but before I could bring my sight to bear, the German wheeled upwards into a steep climbing turn, puffs of black smoke pouring from his exhausts as he did so. Throttle fully open I followed, and nursing my Spitfire around the turn I was able not only to hold him in the climb, but also keep inside his turn and yet slowly but surely close the range. Again he went into a dive, this time by turning over on the inside of his turn, and just at that moment I gave him a quick burst, in desperation really because I couldn't bring my sights to bear, but I hoped it would warn him that I was determined to fight it out. And I was.

By now, charged with the adrenalin of battle, spurred on by increasing confidence in the superiority of my aircraft, I knew that the end result would be dependent on my ability as a pilot not only to stay with the German but to get into a decisive position for the kill. No doubt the German was thinking likewise; he certainly reacted as if he was. From a steep dive into a steep turn and almost immediately into a steep climbing turn in the opposite direction, each manoeuvre following in quick-changing succession. Grimly, determinedly, I hung onto his tail dragging, pulling, bucketing my Spitfire from one impossible firing position to another, rarely being able to bring my guns to bear even for a split second. Sweating from exertion and greying from excessive 'g' I nevertheless managed to keep the 109's heaving belly in sight. A quick, hopeful burst now and again I did manage but with no apparent effect. Whenever I thought I'd got into the ideal position to make a kill, he reacted violently causing me to fire another wasted burst, until eventually there was no answering response from my eight Brownings. I was out of ammunition.

At this juncture I was really close to the 109, so close that I could clearly see the pilot's head darting to the left and to the right as skidding, turning and weaving he tried to keep me in view. He was not to know that I had run out of ammunition, but I had the feeling that he would soon do so, and after savouring the enjoyment of being the hunter, I decided to break off the engagement on my terms before I became the hunted. A quick over-the-shoulder survey revealed an alarmingly distant coastline, and in one violent manoeuvre I pulled viciously on the control column and banked my Spitfire into a diving turn. At the same time I moved the throttle through the 'gate' and, in racing parlance, 'let her go.' A quick glance showed me that the German was not following; either he had been surprised by my quick break-away and couldn't follow or he had had enough, or a bit of both. In the event I was alone in the sky, and I crossed out of France untroubled to return unscathed to Hornchurch.

In my written report on the combat I stated that in my opinion the Spitfire was superior overall to the Me 109, except in the initial climb and dive; however this was an opinion contrary to the belief of the so-called experts. Their judgement was of course based on intelligence assessments and the performance of the 109 in combat with the Hurricane in France. In fact, the Hurricane, though vastly more manoeuvrable than either the Spitfire or the Me 109, was so sadly lacking in speed and rate of climb, that its too-short combat experience against the 109 was not a valid yardstick for comparison. The Spitfire, however, possessed these two attributes to such a degree that, coupled with a better rate of turn than the 109, it had the edge overall in combat. There may have been scepticism by some about my claim for the Spitfire, but I had no doubts on the score; nor did my fellow pilots in 54 Squadron. Later events, particularly in the Battle of Britain, were to prove me right.

For one who has flown most subsequent British fighters, including the supersonic breed, the special place in my heart reserved for the Spitfire has never been seriously challenged. It was my earliest and greatest love. Throughout four years of fighting and 700 combat hours the Spitfire played its part to the full; sadly I sometimes failed to play mine. The fact that I am alive to tell my story, a story whose chapters are made up of crash-landings, mid-air collisons, forced parachute descents, and the ignominy of being blown-up by bombs during take-off, is in no small measure due to the toughness of this great little aircraft whose superiority in performance over all contestants covered up my many deficiencies as a pilot.

I started the war on Spitfires, I ended it flying the same aircraft. I would not have had it any other way.

Post War—Air Commodore Deere

5 FIGHT FOR SURVIVAL
The Battle of Britain

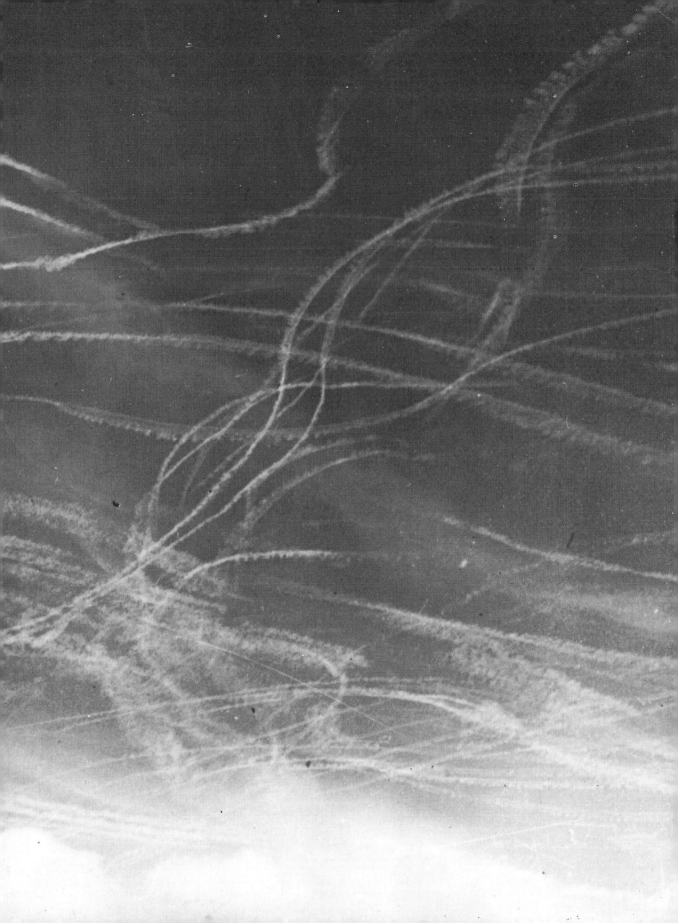

Previous pages: 'The nations'
airy navies grappling in the
central blue': typical Battle of
Britain sky

With the evacuation of the British Expeditionary Force from France through Dunkirk during the last days of May and the first days of June 1940, followed swiftly by the surrender of our French allies, Britain was on her own. The defence of our island kingdom lay in the hands of the Royal Navy and the Royal Air Force.

A dispirited, resentful and beaten British Expeditionary Force had either been taken prisoner by the Germans or evacuated from the Dunkirk beaches and brought home without arms or equipment. It was no fault of these British soldiers that they had been defeated. They had been sent to France ill-trained and ill-equipped to fight the strongest military machine the world had ever seen. Their allies, first the Belgians, then the French, had capitulated and the British were left to fight their way to Dunkirk then home across the Channel.

The Dunkirk evacuation had been covered from the air by the Royal Air Force based in England. So far as Fighter Command was concerned, this was the first combat experience for most of its pilots. The German Luftwaffe pilots by contrast had fought in Spain during the Spanish civil war, in Poland, and in France. They were battle-hardened, confident, had always been numerically and technically superior to their opponents; the possibility of defeat never crossed their minds. '*Wir fahren gegen England*' (We're going against England) they sang as they pre-

Flight of 65 Squadron Spitfires in formation

242 Squadron—Duxford 1940. Left to right: Willie McKnight, the author, Eric Ball

pared to destroy the British air defences in advance of invasion by the German army. Meanwhile they were consolidating their conquest of France and the Low Countries.

There had been Hurricane squadrons in France since the early months of the war. Their pilots had fought against the Me 109 and the German twin-engined bombers, and of course the Ju 87 dive-bomber. One would have thought that the views and experiences of these pilots would have been passed on to the Hurricane and Spitfire pilots of England-based squadrons so that we would have had some first-hand information about the tactics of the German fighter pilots, the armament and vulnerability of the German bombers, and the most effective method of dealing with them. Not a bit of it. We never heard a word between the Dunkirk period and the lull before the start of the Battle of Britain in July, although a number of these pilots were by then back in this country. This was no reflection on them because they had written combat reports and probably reported their views many times about specific tactics. It merely showed a total lack of understanding of basic operational needs by the non-operational, non-flying officers and personnel at headquarters.

The result was that most of us whose total combat experience was at Dunkirk, which was a unique type of operation against limited Luftwaffe resistance, had to work out our own methods of combating the total strength of the German Luftwaffe.

Luckily for us, the Germans made more mistakes than we did. And it is relevant that the Luftwaffe had so far met no serious resistance in their short history, particularly in the quality of their opponents. As a result, they were over-confident. When their hitherto successful 'blitzkrieg' methods failed, they were firstly puzzled, then unsure of themselves, and finally lost confidence in their leadership, which undermined the morale of their pilots and aircrew. On our side, we were nearly all new to the game, especially our headquarters' staffs and operations rooms' controllers. We learned quickly. Perhaps most important of all we were fighting in our own sky over our own country. There is no greater incentive.

I had taken over 242 Squadron on 24 June 1940. We were based at Coltishall, just north of Norwich in Norfolk.

The Squadron had been formed at the beginning of the war. It was composed almost exclusively of Canadians serving in the Royal Air Force (the Royal Canadian Air Force units had not yet arrived in England); it was designated 242 (Canadian) Fighter Squadron R.A.F.

The Squadron had spent some time in France at the beginning of 1940, had much combat experience, sustained some casualties, and finally had to fly back to England minus a Squadron Commander and both Flight Commanders.

It did not take me long to get this Squadron into first-class shape.

They could all fly the Hurricane and most of them had fired their guns at an enemy. I acquired two English Flight Commanders of my own choosing, Eric Ball and George Powell-Sheddon. George had no combat experience; Eric had an extra wide parting down the middle of his hair as a reminder of the Me 109 which nearly got him at Dunkirk. As for me, I had had a few casual squirts at fleeting targets during the Dunkirk evacuation, and accounted for a Me 109 whose pilot must have been as inexperienced as I was, since he appeared in front of me and continued in that position while I shot him down. I had also silenced one German rear-gunner.

We three with our vast total of inexperience were dedicated to reforming and reactivating the Squadron decimated in France in time for Hitler's assault against the British Isles.

In the Squadron (mainly Canadian) was an English Pilot Officer, Denis Crowley-Milling. He was posted to my wing at Tangmere in 1941 and was shot down just after I was. He was not picked up by the Germans and escaped via Spain back to England to continue a distinguished career in the Royal Air Force. He is now Air Marshal Sir Denis Crowley-Milling. Amongst the Canadians were Flying Officers like Stan Turner, Bob Grassick, and Willie McKnight, all of whom had considerable fighting experience behind them against the Luftwaffe. Willie McKnight already wore the ribbon of the Distinguished

The other side of the channel—
1940. German bombs for
England; German aircrew;
and the Luftwaffe commander
Goering

There is a splendid anecdote
about the outstanding German
fighter leader, Adolf Galland.
After the Luftwaffe's failure in
the Battle of Britain,
Reichsmarschal Hermann
Goering (left, centre) assembled
all the fighter leaders and
accused them of failing to
defend properly the German
bombers from the British
fighters. Indeed he virtually
accused them of cowardice.
Galland, then a Major, lost his
temper and, so the story goes,
removed his Iron Cross and
placed it on the table saying he
would not wear it again until
the Herr Reichsmarschal
withdrew the accusation.
Goering, having thrown his
tantrum, then turned on the
charm and asked Galland to
say what he wanted and he
should have it. Bloody-minded
to the last Galland answered,
'A staffel of Spitfires'

Flying Cross for his prowess in the French skies.

I had spent the first days on concentrated flying training in the shape of flight- and squadron-formation manoeuvres and so on.

By the first week in July the Squadron was fully operational and raring to go.

On 11 July came my lucky encounter with the Dornier (described in Chapter 1). We spent most of July patrolling convoys on the east coast and being sent off on interceptions only to find they were friendly aircraft from nearby squadrons of Blenheims.

The Battle of Britain lasted officially from 1 July to 31 October 1940. The heavy fighting occurred from 8 August until 21 September.

In July, over the Goodwin Sands, Alan Deere's Spitfire collided with a Me 109 during a dog-fight. This is what he had to say later:

'Black smoke poured into the cockpit and flames appeared from the engine. I reached to open the hood in order to bale out, only to discover that his propeller had struck the front of my windscreen and the whole fixture was so twisted that I could not move the hood. I could not see for smoke, but managed to ascertain that I was headed inland. Nearly blinded and choked, I succeeded in keeping the airspeed at about 100 miles an hour. The engine had now seized and I just waited to hit the ground. Suddenly there was a terrific jerk and I was tossed left, then right, and finally pitched hard forward on my straps, which fortunately held fast. I seemed to plough through all sorts of things and then stop.

'The remains of my ammunition were going off in a series of pops and the flames were getting very near the cockpit. I practically broke open the hood and, undoing my harness, ran to a safe distance. My eyebrows were singed. Both my knees were bruised, but otherwise I was uninjured. The Spitfire was blazing furiously in the middle of a cornfield and had left a trail of broken posts and pieces of wing plus the complete tail unit, extending for 200 yards.'

The first important phase of the Battle of Britain was from 8–18 August. Hundreds of enemy bombers, escorted by fighters attacked shipping and ports on the south-east and south coasts between the North Foreland and Portland. On 8 August, a total of 160 enemy aircraft attacked a convoy off the Isle of Wight, sinking two ships. In the afternoon, more than 130 went for another convoy off Bournemouth.

The enemy came back to the attack three days later by bombing Portland and Weymouth, as well as going for further convoys in the Thames Estuary and off Harwich. Although their

Bombs in the sea—flak in the sky. Dover, 29 July

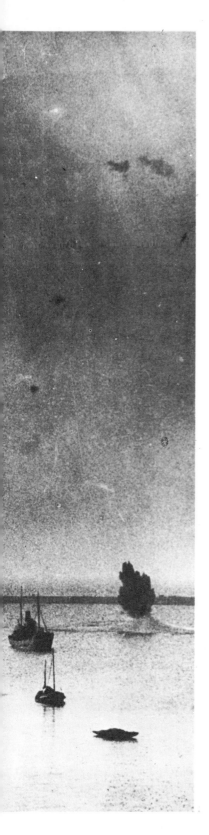

Stukas proved no equal to Hurricanes, the dive-bombers did some damage to the two ports, which encouraged Reichmarshal Goering, Commander of the Luftwaffe, to launch about 200 aircraft in eleven waves against Dover. On the same day, 150 headed farther west for the Portsmouth and Isle of Wight area, but by this time the enemy losses had soared.

Pilot Officer Stevenson of 74 Squadron was one of those who met the Luftwaffe hordes over Dover. This is what happened to him after sighting a Me 109:

'I climbed up to him. He must have thought I was a Me 109 but when he suddenly dived away I followed him and gave him a two-second deflection burst. The E/A [enemy aircraft] lurched slightly and went into a vertical dive. I kept my height at 15,000 feet and watched. I saw the E/A dive straight into the sea fifteen miles south-east of Dover and disappear in a big splash . . .

'I then climbed to 23,000 feet up-sun and saw a formation of twelve Me 109s 2,000 feet beneath me, proceeding north of Dover. It was my intention to attach myself to the back of this formation from out of the sun, and spray the whole formation. As I was diving for them, a really large volume of cannon and machine-gun fire came from behind. There were about twelve Me 109s diving at me from the sun and at least half of them must have been firing deflection shots at me. There was a popping noise and my control column became useless. I found myself doing a vertical dive, getting faster and faster.

'I pulled the hood back, I got my head out of the cockpit and the slipstream tore the rest of me clean out of the machine. My trouser leg and both shoes were torn off. I saw my machine crash into the sea a mile off Deal. It took me twenty minutes to come down. I had been drifting eleven miles out to sea. One string of my parachute did not come undone and I was dragged along by my left leg at ten miles an hour with my head underneath the water. After three minutes, I was almost unconscious, when the string came undone. I got my breath back and started swimming. There was a heavy sea running.

'After one and a half hours, an MTB came to look for me. I fired my revolver at it. It went out of sight, but came back. I changed magazines and fired all my shots over it. It heard my shots and I kicked up a foam in the water, and it saw me. It then picked me up and took me to Dover!'

Despite the large losses sustained by the enemy, they attacked again, this time Portsmouth on 13 and 15 August. In some of these raids, particularly one timed at soon after 5 p.m. on 15 August, the Germans used between 300 and 400 aircraft.

By then the enemy was beginning to realize that our fighter force was much stronger than they had imagined. It was evidently time to take drastic action to try to put the R.A.F. opposition out of commission. So while still stepping up attacks on south-coast towns, they made an all-out assault on fighter aerodromes in the south and south-east of England: Dover, Deal, Hawkinge, Lympne, Martlesham, Manston, Croydon, Detling, Kenley and Biggin Hill all were attacked—some several times.

Once more the Luftwaffe could hardly fail to do damage—but the price they paid for these results was becoming too high for them. On that first of the fateful days of this new phase—15 August—the original reckoning of raiders destroyed came to no fewer than 180.

Nevertheless, the Germans remained as determined as ever. They returned to the attack, throwing in 500 to 600 aircraft on 16 August. The enemy flew in the proportion of one bomber to every three fighters: clearly a lesson had been learned. But they had only half-learned the lesson—that the most formidable aeroplane in the sky is a single-seater, one-engined, front-gun fighter. It will out-fly and out-fight anything else in the sky except another of its own kind. The Germans did indeed send more fighters with their bombers, but a number of these were twin-engined Me 110s which were quite fast but lightly built and easy meat for a Spitfire or Hurricane. They used to fly alongside the bombers. The Germans later used them as night-fighters quite effectively.

The main targets around this time were more fighter aerodromes: Rochester, Kenley, Croydon, Biggin Hill, Manston, West Malling, Gosport, Northolt and Tangmere. In these two climactic days of the first phase, enemy losses again proved to be high.

During this period the armament experts at Fighter Command had been trying to improve the weight of fire-power of the Spitfire and had decided that two 20-mm cannons plus four machine guns would be an ideal mixture. 19 Squadron—the first squadron of all to have Spitfires—were the unlucky recipients of these first cannons.

I well remember the occasion when 19 Squadron's Spitfires were fitted with these cannons, since we were on the same aerodrome, Duxford. The cannons would fire about two rounds and then stop. The reason was that the wings had been adapted to accept cannons instead of being built *for* cannons. The stoppage occurred on recoil. After a couple of sorties with no cannons working in close combat with the enemy, the pilots were not best pleased. The armament 'experts' at 12 Group and Fighter Command tried to insist that the 19 Squadron armourers did not know their job. 'Stuffy' Dowding heard about this and came, with his armament 'experts' to see for himself.

I was present on this occasion. Sandy Lane was the 19 Squadron Commander, an old chum. Dowding said: 'Hullo, Lane, I hear you're in trouble with your cannons. Tell me.' Sandy replied: 'They fire one round, sir, and that's all.' At this point one of the armament 'experts' mistakenly intervened to say: 'There's nothing wrong with the cannons, sir, I think the armourers do not fully understand them.' Courteously, Dowding turned to him and said: 'I want to hear what Squadron Leader Lane thinks.' He looked at Sandy and said: 'What do you recommend?' Without pause, Sandy answered: 'Remove the cannons and put back the machine guns, sir.' Stuffy said: 'Thank you, Lane.' He then turned to his staff and said: 'You will arrange that straightaway, please.'

That was typical of the C.-in-C. Fighter Command in 1940. I was present once when he told one of his staff officers: 'Our job in this Headquarters is to look after the squadrons in the field.' The following year when the Spitfire Vb was in production the wing had been designed to take cannons and they worked perfectly.

To return to the fighting of these August days, Flight Lieutenant James Brindley Nicolson of 249 Squadron, provided this experience:

Answering a scramble signal, he thrust his Hurricane along the runway and into the air. He had always shown terrific enthusiasm for air fighting and now, in his first engagement, his skill would at last be tested. He was impatient to get at the enemy—like so many of us!

The white con trails looked like random brush strokes on a canvas sky, as he went into action over Southampton and the Isle of Wight. The wave of enemy bombers was accompanied by the usual fighter escort of Me 109s. Nicolson was told to deal with the fighters. He turned his section of Hurricanes and made contact. As he was lining up the enemy in his sights he was caught from behind by another Me 109. Cannon shells ploughed into the Hurricane's cockpit injuring one of Nicolson's eyes and damaging a foot. The gravity petrol-tank was pierced, and petrol poured into the front end of the cockpit. This was ignited by the heat of the engine. Flames spread. Both the cockpit and the pilot were alight. Nicolson reached to slide back the canopy. As he did so and prepared to jump, he saw a Messerschmitt in front of him. He stayed in the cockpit, took hold of the stick again, and groped for the rudder bar with his feet. He hardly knew what he was doing. The whole of the lower part of the fighter was aflame. Somehow Nicolson kept his concentration and sighted himself on the enemy. With a wounded eye, up to his waist in flames, his hands blistering on the controls, he battled on until his range closed enough to be entirely accurate. He fired.

A stream of bullets tore at the enemy. The Messerschmitt reeled away and spiralled towards the ground. But Nicolson was still in a furnace. He struggled out, pulled his ripcord and then fainted, landing unconscious just outside Southampton, with bad burns on his hands, face, neck and legs. They rushed him to the nearest hospital, where he hung between life and death for two days and nights. He was awarded the only V.C. of the Battle of Britain.

Then followed recovery, recuperation, and back to flying. As Wing Commander Nicolson he never saw final victory, for he died in a Liberator crash in the Bay of Bengal, just before the war ended.

Another account of this phase comes from Flying Officer E. S. Marrs:

'I got in a burst of about three seconds when—crash! The whole world seemed to be tumbling in on me. I pushed the stick forward hard, went into a vertical dive and held it until I was below cloud. I had a look round.

'The chief trouble was that petrol was gushing into the cockpit at the rate of gallons all over my feet, and there was a sort of lake of petrol in the bottom of the cockpit. My knee and legs were tingling all over as if I had pushed them into a bed of nettles. There was a hole in the side of the cockpit where a bullet had come in and hit the dashboard, knocking away the starter button. Another bullet, I think an explosive one, had knocked away one of my petrol taps in front of the joystick, spattering my leg with little splinters and sending a chunk of something through the backside of my petrol tank near the bottom. I had obviously run into some pretty good cross-fire from Heinkels.

'I made for home at top speed to get there before all my petrol ran out. I was about fifteen miles from the aerodrome and it was a heart-rending business with all the petrol gushing over my legs and the constant danger of fire. About five miles from the 'drome, smoke began to come from under the dashboard. I thought the whole thing might blow up at any minute, so I switched off my engine. The smoke stopped.

'I glided towards the 'drome and tried putting my wheels down. One came down and the other remained stuck up. I tried to get the one that was down up again! It was stuck down! There was nothing for it but to make a one-wheel landing.

'I switched on my engine again to make the aerodrome. It took me some way and then began to smoke again, so I hastily switched off. I was now near enough and made a normal approach and held off. I made a good landing, touching down lightly. The unsupported wing slowly began to drop. I was able to hold it up for some time and then down came the wing-tip on the ground. I began to slew round and counteracted as much as possible with the brake on the wheel which was down. I ended up going sideways on one wheel, a tail-wheel and a wing-tip. Luckily the good tyre held out and the only damage to the aeroplane, apart from that done by the bullets, was a wing-tip which is easily replaceable. I hopped out and went off to the M.O. to get a lot of metal splinters picked out of my leg and wrist. I felt jolly glad to be down on the ground without having caught fire . . .'

On 18 August, in an evening attack on the Thames estuary, a squadron of Hurricanes shot down nearly their own number without loss in just fifty minutes.

Squadrons of the Auxiliary Air Force were fighting side by side with the Royal Air Force. For instance, six A.A.F. Squadrons flew Spitfires: 602 (City of Glasgow), 603 (City of Edinburgh), 609 (West Riding), 610 (County of Chester), 611 (West Lancashire) and 616 (South Yorkshire).

After the eleven days from 8–18 August, Goering withdrew to rest his pilots, lick his wounds and count the cost: losses to the tune of 367 aircraft destroyed. In the same period, Fighter Command lost 183 aircraft in combat and 30 more on the ground. On 20 August, Winston Churchill spoke those wonderful words in the House of Commons:

'Never in the field of human conflict was so much owed by so many to so few.'

Then the second phase started: the attack on inland aerodromes. Goering learned some lessons from the first defeat and changed tactics. Fighter escorts increased; the size of bomber formations decreased; and there were other technical changes.

I lost my first young pilot on 20 August—Midshipman Patterson, shot down into the sea on a convoy patrol. With Fighter Com-

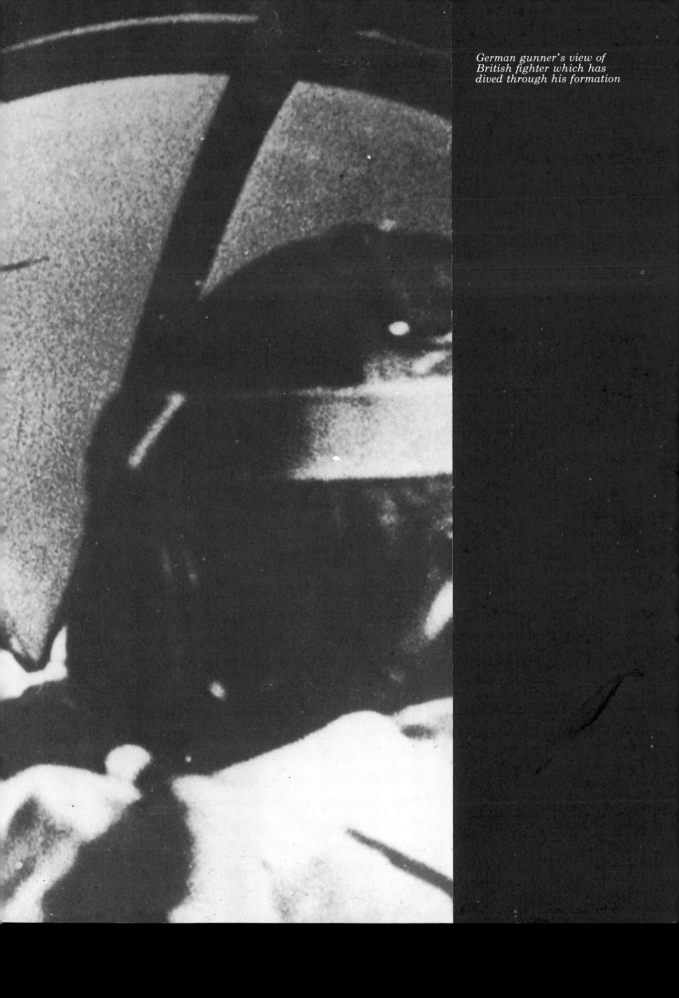

German gunner's view of
British fighter which has
dived through his formation

Gun camera pictures from a Hurricane or Spitfire showing destruction of Me 110s. Far right: Spitfire in trouble, seen from German bomber

mand short of pilots in the frantic build-up after Dunkirk, the Royal Navy seconded to us fighter pilots from the Fleet Air Arm. They were without exception well-trained, disciplined and great characters. I had three in 242 Squadron—Midshipman Patterson, and Sub-Lieutenants Cork and Gardner. The first two were R.N. while Jimmy Gardner (the sole survivor of the war) was 'Wavy-Navy' (R.N.V.R.). The part played by pilots of the Royal Navy in the Battle of Britain is never forgotten by the rest of us.

From 19–23 August, things were relatively quiet, but on 24 August, the enemy made renewed attacks on Manston, North Weald, Portsmouth, and Ramsgate. The score was 38–22 in our favour. At 6.45 p.m. on that evening, 110 enemy aeroplanes were intercepted—but they turned and fled before they could be engaged. In fact, during this next phase, 24 August–5 September, the Luftwaffe unleashed some thirty-five major attacks on inland fighter aerodromes and aircraft factories—also bombing big residential districts in Kent, the Thames Estuary and Essex.

From 24–29 August, Portland, Dover, and Manston were all pounded, as well as other targets, and fierce fighting was seen over the North Foreland, Gravesend, and Deal. During one such attack on 25 August, twenty aircraft were shot down—a dozen of them by Spitfires of 602 Squadron. The location of this encounter was near Portland. Portsmouth and Southampton proved to be the principal targets on that day, but the Luftwaffe also made heavy assaults in the Dover–Folkestone area, as well as over the Thames and Kent generally.

On 29 August, Flying Officer Richard Hillary of 603 Squadron pressed the button to fire a burst at a Me 109 as it crossed his sights for a fraction of a second. He did not get the Me 109, so he scanned the sky for his own Spitfires. Instead he happened on a Hurricane squadron flying in a trio of vic ('v') formations. They did not seem to have any protection, so he attached himself to them as a self-appointed 'tail-end Charlie'.

Then bullets began to hit his port wing. Smoke belched out of his engine, so he thought quickly and aimed towards Lympne. As the engine might give out at any moment, he then thought better of it and settled for a Kent cornfield where he made a passable landing—at any rate good enough to allow him to climb from the Spitfire cockpit.

This gallant officer was shot down on September 3 and badly wounded. He parachuted into the sea and was picked up by the Margate lifeboat. He recovered from his wounds and returned to combat but died later flying at night. He was the author of *The Last Enemy*, one of the best books to come out of World War II. His name lives.

On 30 August, the attack was suddenly switched to inland fighter aerodromes. No fewer than 800 aircraft darkened the skies of southern England in an effort to neutralize the key airfields of Kenley, North Weald, Hornchurch, Debden, Lympne,

Detling, Duxford, Northolt, and Biggin Hill.

German raid on Portland in August

By 6 September, the Germans either believed that they had struck sufficiently at the fighter stations, or else they were following a prearranged timetable to switch their attack again, for on 7 September they opened the third phase of the Battle of Britain—aimed at London. All this time, too, the threat existed of invasion by the enemy, but the British were gradually beginning to believe that this could not materialize without complete air superiority—which the Germans so far had failed to achieve.

After hammering away throughout 6 September against inland fighter stations, next day the Luftwaffe launched an enormous effort to reach London and destroy the docks. These onslaughts aimed at the capital came in two or three distinct waves at intervals of about twenty minutes, the whole thing lasting nearly an hour. Waves of twenty to forty bombers throbbed towards London, with fighter forces in close escort. Extra protection came from large groups of fighters flying at higher altitudes: up to about 26,000 feet in a clear sky, making the task of the Observer Corps extremely difficult.

Somewhere between the coast and London, usually in the Edenbridge–Tunbridge Wells area, but sometimes nearer the sea, the air forces met. Spitfires took the high-flying fighter screen; Hurricanes engaged the fighter escort; other Hurricanes flew hellbent for the bombers. Dog-fights developed all over the Kent skies. For a few minutes at a time, the air was vibrant with distant machine-gun fire, with a background noise of the faint roar of hundreds of engines, sometimes swelling to a crescendo as a wounded aircraft screamed to earth.

Occasionally, watchers saw sprays of parachutes blossoming in the blue sky. The warm September sun shone on more and more wrecks of the Luftwaffe, bearing on their broken wings, to use Mr Churchill's famous phrase, 'the crooked cross of Nazi infamy'.

On August 30, 242 Squadron, which I commanded, had had a successful first engagement with the Luftwaffe under favourable circumstances. Although, as was usual in 1940, heavily outnumbered, we had the height, the sun, and controlled the fight. We felt that with more aeroplanes we would have been even more successful.

So, after this initial success, the idea of a wing of three squadrons was born. The Czech 310 Squadron (Hurricanes) commanded by Bill Blackwood with two British flight-commanders was posted to Duxford. 19 Squadron (Spitfires) was there anyhow, commanded by Sandy Lane, a fine leader and pilot.

The wing first went into action on 7 September. We had been greatly looking forward to our first formation of thirty-six fighters going into action together, but we were unlucky. We were alerted late, and were underneath the bombers and their fighter escorts when we met fifteen miles north of the Thames. All we could do was attack them as best we could while 19 Squadron tried to hold off assaults from the Me 109s. Some of the Spitfires and indeed the Hurricanes were caught on the climb by the German fighters, but our casualties were less than might have been expected.

To be attacked by an enemy fighter when you are climbing is fatal if your opponent is experienced. You are flying slowly and are thus virtually unmanoeuvrable as well as being a sitting target for an opponent above you and flying faster. I lost one pilot killed, a second shot down but unhurt, a third untouched but his Hurricane badly shot up, while the C.O. (myself) got a cockpit-full of bullets and the right aileron shot off his Hurricane. We destroyed eleven aircraft, but it was windy work, let there be no mistake. On landing, I rang the Operations Room in a fury to be told that we had been sent off as soon as 11 Group had called for us from Duxford. This was one of the recurring problems during this heavy last period of the Battle. 11 Group which guarded the south-east of England was nearest to the enemy operating from northern France. Its controllers had an impossible task. When the German armadas started across the Channel for London, half or more of 11 Group's airfields were too close

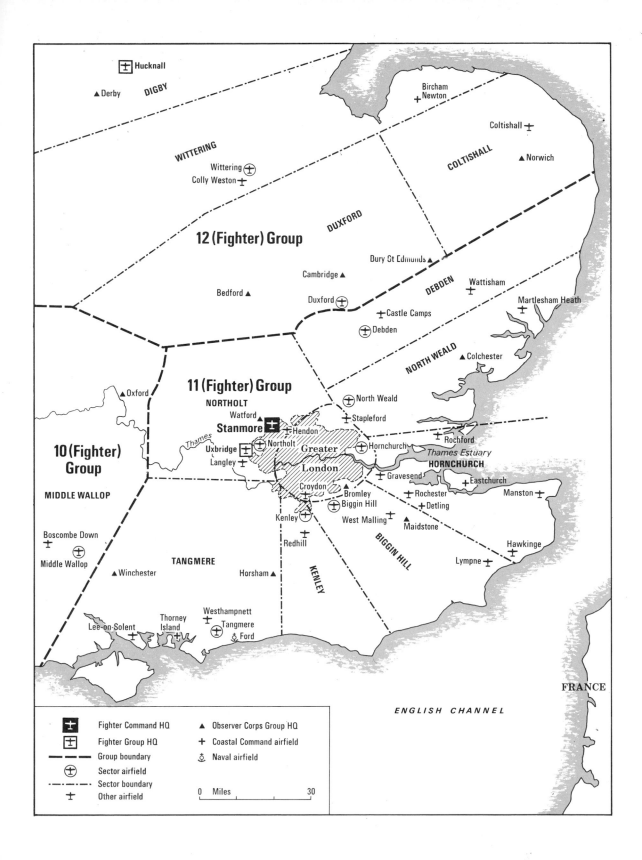

Hucknall

▲ Derby   **DIGBY**

Bircham
Newton +

Coltishall +

WITTERING

Wittering ⊕
Colly Weston +

COLTISHALL

▲ Norwich

DUXFORD

12 (Fighter) Group

Bury St Edmunds ▲

Cambridge ▲

Wattisham

Bedford ▲

Duxford ⊕

DEBDEN

Martlesham Heath

+ Castle Camps
⊕ Debden

NORTH WEALD

▲ Colchester

▲ Oxford

11 (Fighter) Group

NORTHOLT

Watford ▲

Stanmore ✈

⊕ North Weald
+ Stapleford

+ Hendon

**10 (Fighter)
Group**

Uxbridge ⊞
Langley +

Northolt ⊕

**Greater
London**

⊕ Hornchurch

Rochford +

Thames Estuary

HORNCHURCH

Thames

MIDDLE WALLOP

Croydon +

+ Gravesend

▲ Bromley

⊕ Biggin Hill

+ Rochester
+ Detling

+ Eastchurch

Manston +

Kenley ⊕

West Malling +

▲ Maidstone

Boscombe Down +

Middle Wallop ⊕

TANGMERE

▲ Winchester

Redhill +

Horsham ▲

BIGGIN HILL

KENLEY

Hawkinge +

Lympne +

Westhampnett +
⊕ Tangmere

⚓ Ford

Thorney
Island +

Lee-on-Solent +

FRANCE

ENGLISH CHANNEL

✈	Fighter Command HQ	▲	Observer Corps Group HQ
⊞	Fighter Group HQ	+	Coastal Command airfield
— — —	Group boundary	⚓	Naval airfield
⊕	Sector airfield		
—·—·—	Sector boundary		
+	Other airfield		

0   Miles   30

for the fighters to gain height to intercept the enemy, with the result that their pilots had to climb northwards. Duxford was forty-three miles north of Tilbury, an ideal position for intercepting an enemy approaching London from eighty miles southeast of our capital. Quite naturally, the 11 Group controllers, who bore the heaviest burden of responsibility during the Battle of Britain, committed all their own squadrons before calling on Duxford in 12 Group.

After one or two of these sorties with the three squadrons, two more were eventually added making the Duxford Wing—as it was called—five squadrons of sixty fighters. The two extra squadrons were the Polish 302 (Hurricanes) and the Auxiliary 610 (Spitfires). We thus had three Hurricane squadrons which flew together at the lower level (20,000 feet if we were called in time) with the Spitfires protecting us 5,000 feet higher. It worked like a charm once or twice, and the arrival of this large formation in support of hard-pressed 11 Group squadrons was highly satisfactory. Unfortunately it was too seldom.

During this period of mass formation raids, the methods of attack adopted by the British fighter leaders were decided according to the situation. There were one or two rare occasions when a leader found himself approaching an enemy formation head-on at the same height. This was a splendid moment for the leading section of fighters because the enemy bomber crews were sitting in a 'glass-house' [see colour illustration on page 108] in the front end, with no protection. Facing an eight-gun fighter. The worst sufferer in this respect was the Heinkel 111 which had three people in the front consisting of two pilots and a gunner lying on his stomach between them—the latter had to manipulate a single machine-gun which fired out of the nose. Both the Spitfire and the Hurricane were each so instantly responsive to the pilot's whim that this hazardous head-on attack was perfectly possible since, having fired a short burst, the pilot pulled up over the bomber.

Tactics were not for the Battle of Britain. All the fighter pilots could do was to get at the German bombers the quickest way possible, risking interference from Me 109s. These enemy fighters took a heavy toll particularly of 11 Group squadrons based in Kent and Surrey which were too near the Channel to climb to the enemy height in time. As a result they were frequently clobbered on the way up.

The concentrated daylight attacks on London had started at the beginning of September with the heaviest raids occurring on the 7th, 10th, 11th, 12th, 13th, and of course the 15th.

About this time a Spitfire pilot made a memorable observation which must be recorded. Around 5 p.m. on September 7, 350 bombers and fighters arrived in two waves. They penetrated east of Croydon to the Thames Estuary and further north where we intercepted them from Duxford. This young British pilot

▶ 89

Spitfires Mark Vb

Spitfires Mark IXc
returning from a
sortie south of
Rome

**Hurricane Mark IIs
in the desert**

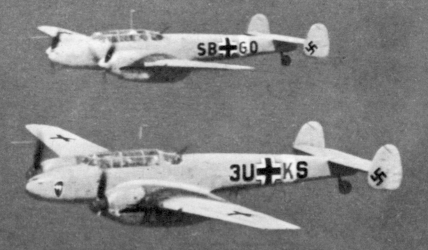

Two Me 110s in the
Mediterranean

Ju 87s being
bombed up

Me 110s over France

Left below: **Western Desert. Me 109 sighting his guns**

Left above: **Focke-Wulf 190s – for a brief period this radial-engined fighter outflew the Spitfire**

Pilots of the Australian 453 Squadron, May 1944. They flew Spitfire IXbs

A.T.A. pilot with Spitfire Mark IX. These girls did a wonderful job ferrying to the squadrons anything from a four-engined Lancaster bomber to a Spitfire

remarked that there were so many enemy fighters layered up to 30,000 feet that it was 'just like looking up the escalator at Piccadilly Circus'.

On September 13 a Heinkel 111 bombed Buckingham Palace. Unfortunately for the German, a single experienced Hurricane pilot, Flight Sergeant 'Ginger' Lacey, shot him down in weather so poor that Lacey could not make his way home. He climbed up in the cloud and baled out. Lacey, still almost a boy at the time, had a remarkable Battle of Britain record. He destroyed eighteen enemy aircraft during the Battle.

15 September 1940 was the day that the Battle was won. It was a Sunday. In the south-east the day dawned a little misty, but cleared by 8 a.m. to disclose light cumulus cloud at 2,000 to 3,000 feet. The extent of this cloud varied, and in places it was heavy enough to produce light local showers. But visibility remained good on the whole, with a slight westerly wind shifting to north-west.

The first enemy patrols arrived soon after 9 a.m. They were reported over the Straits of Dover, the Thames Estuary, off Harwich, and between Lympne and Dungeness. Their common goal: London.

This force comprised Dornier 17s and 215s escorted by Me 109s. They flew at various heights between 15,000–26,000 feet. From the ground they looked like black dots, some trailing long streamers of white vapour; from the air like model aeroplanes which rapidly became larger as we approached.

Battle commenced, and it raged for about three-quarters of an hour over east Kent and London. A hundred bombers or so burst through to reach the eastern and southern quarters of the capital. A number of them were intercepted above the centre of the city itself, just as Big Ben was striking the hour of noon.

The air over south-east England was one colossal battlefield, from the Thames Estuary to Dover, from London to the coast.

Individual and collective fights erupted all over the sky. The whole scene was described exactly in the astonishingly accurate prophecy of the Poet Laureate Tennyson who died in 1892. In his poem 'Locksley Hall' he wrote:
'For I dip't into the future, far as human eye could see,
Saw the vision of the world, and all the wonder that would
    be . . .
Heard the heavens fill with shouting, and there rain'd a
    ghastly dew
From the nations' airy navies grappling in the central blue.'

To understand the nature of this Battle it must be made clear that it was a concentration of attacking and defending aircraft fighting over an area of England inside a straight line drawn from Norwich in Norfolk to Portland in Dorset. The aeroplanes involved were flying at speeds of 220 250 m.p.h., and sometimes faster. Once the enemy was intercepted and a large formation

scattered, running battles between two or more aeroplanes continued all over the sky. Combat reports of British pilots would read 'attacked enemy from Hammersmith to Dungeness' or 'attack delivered from London to the French coast'. Such attacks might start and be pressed home at any height from 25,000 feet down to near the ground. There could be as many as 140 separate fights going on at the same time in this cuboid of sky. One moment the sky was full, the next you were apparently alone in the heavens.

That morning, sixteen squadrons of 11 Group, followed by five each from 10 and 12 Groups, took off to engage the enemy. All but one of these squadrons in the battle came face to face with the Luftwaffe very soon after taking to the sky. Five squadrons of Spitfires opened their attack against the oncoming hordes of Huns over the Maidstone–Canterbury–Dover–Dungeness area. These were in action slightly before the Hurricane squadrons, which intercepted further back, between Maidstone, Tunbridge Wells, and London.

The R.A.F. found the enemy flying in various types of formations. The bombers were usually some thousands of feet below 'the fighters, but sometimes this position was reversed. The bombers flew either in 'Vics' of from five to seven aircraft, in lines of five aircraft abreast, or in a diamond pattern. The Me 109s were usually in Vics. One pilot saw the enemy as attacking in little groups of nine, arranged in threes like a sergeant's stripes. Each group of nine was supported by nine Me 110 fighters with single-seater Me 109s or He 113s circling high above.

On ground radios the German pilots could be heard calling out to each other over their wireless phones:

Achtung! Schpitfeuer.

With good cause. Our pilots opened fire at an average range of 200 yards, closing sometimes to less than fifty yards. Many of the enemy fighters belonged to the readily-identifiable Yellow-Nose squadrons. We always thought they were special, until others appeared with different coloured noses—blue, red, white, or sometimes two colours! Then we realized they were just different squadron identification colours. Once the battle was joined, the pilots lost formation utterly, and each one chose individual enemy aircraft.

It was a fast-moving, ever-changing combat, demanding the utmost alertness. One pilot dived out of the sun on to an Me 109 which blew up after receiving his first burst of fire. By this time he found that another Me 109 was on his tail. He turned, got it in his sights, and set it on fire. As he had become parted from his comrades, he started to return to base. Just as he was coming down, he received a message saying that the enemy were above. He looked up, saw a group of Dorniers at 14,000 feet, climbed, and attacked them. He got in a burst at one of them, which crashed into a wood and exploded.

The assault on London. Overleaf: German bomber over the Thames

91

While Spitfires and Hurricanes were in action over Kent, other Hurricanes were dealing with those of the enemy who, by sheer strength of numbers, had broken through to London's outskirts. Fourteen squadrons of Hurricanes, almost at once reinforced by three more of Spitfires, took up this challenge, all of them coming into action between noon and twenty past twelve. Then followed an engagement extending all the way from London to the coast—and beyond.

A Squadron Leader describes the morning fighting:

'The day dawned bright and clear at Croydon. It never seemed to do anything else during those exciting weeks of August and September. But to us it was just another day. We weren't interested in Hitler's entry into London; most of us were wondering whether we should have time to finish breakfast before the first blitz started. We were lucky.

'It wasn't till 9.30 that the sirens started wailing and the order came through to rendezvous base at 20,000 feet. As we were climbing in a southerly direction at 15,000 feet, we saw 30 Heinkels supported by 50 Me 109s 4,000 feet above them, and 20 Me 110s to the flank, approaching us from above. We turned and climbed, flying in the same direction as the bombers, with the whole squadron strung out in echelon to port up-sun, so that each man had a view of the enemy.

' "A" Flight timed their attack to perfection, coming down-sun in a power dive on the enemy's left flank. As each was selecting his own man, the Me 110 escort streamed in to intercept with cannons blazing at 1,000 yards' range, but they were two seconds too late—too late to engage our fighters, but just in time to make them hesitate long enough to miss the bomber leader. Two Heinkels keeled out of the formation.

'Meanwhile, the Me 110s had flashed out of sight, leaving the way clear for "B" Flight, as long as the Me 109s stayed above. "B" Flight leader knew how to bide his time, but just as he was about to launch his attack, the Heinkels did the unbelievable thing. They turned south, into the sun, and into him.

'With his first burst the leader destroyed the leading bomber which blew up with such force that it knocked a wing off the left-hand bomber. A little bank and a burst from his guns sent the right hand Heinkel out of the formation with smoke pouring from both engines. Before returning home, he knocked down a Me 109. Four aircraft destroyed for an expenditure of 1,200 rounds was the best justification of our new tactics.'

A glimpse of the battle at noon is provided by a Hurricane Squadron Leader:

'The bombers were coming in towards London from the southeast and at first we could not tell how many there were. We opened our throttles and started to climb up towards them, aiming for a point well ahead, where we expected to contact them at their own height. As we converged I saw that there were

about twenty of them, and it looked as though it was going to be a nice party, for the other squadrons of Hurricanes and Spitfires also turned to join in. By the time we reached a position near the bombers, we were over London—central London, I should say. We had gained a little height on them, too, so when I gave the order to attack we were able to dive on them from their right.

'Each of us selected his own target. Our first attack broke them up pretty nicely. The Dornier I attacked with a burst lasting several seconds began to turn to the left away from his friends. I gave him five seconds, and he went away with white smoke streaming behind him. As I broke away and started to make a steep-climbing turn, I looked over the side. I recognized the river immediately below me through a hole in the clouds. I saw the bends and the bridges and idly wondered where I was. Then I saw Kennington Oval and I thought to myself, "That is where they play cricket".

'I soon found myself below another Dornier which had white smoke coming from it. It was being attacked by two Hurricanes and a Spitfire and was travelling north and turning slightly to the right. As I could not see anything else to attack at that moment, I climbed above him and did a diving attack. Coming into the attack I noticed what appeared to be a red light shining in the rear-gunner's cockpit, but when I got closer I realized I was looking right through the gunner's cockpit into the pilot and observer's cockpit beyond. The red light was fire. I gave it a quick burst and as I passed him on the right I looked in through the big glass nose of the Dornier. It was like a furnace inside.

'He began to go down, and we watched. In a few seconds the tail came off, and the bomber did a forward somersault and then went into a spin. After he had done two turns in his spin, his wings broke off outboard of the engines, so that all that was left, as the blazing aircraft fell, was half a fuselage and the wing-roots with the engines on their ends. This dived straight down, just past the edge of a cloud, and then the cloud got in the way, and I could see no more of him.

'The battle was over by then. I couldn't see anything else to shoot at so I flew home. Our squadron's score was five certainties.

A Flight Sergeant of 504 Squadron attacked three Dorniers. From the first, which he hit, he got a spray of enemy oil over his windscreen, practically blacking out his vision. Then he went for a second Dornier, which he set on fire. And the third time he went one better, for he suddenly saw a parachute flapping out of the aeroplane. Suddenly his Hurricane went out of control into a spin, either caused by collision with an enemy or for some other reason. All he knew was that it was spinning terrifyingly and then he was in cloud, and trapped in the cockpit.

Once through the clouds, he struggled against all the various strains acting on his body, and flung himself into what seemed

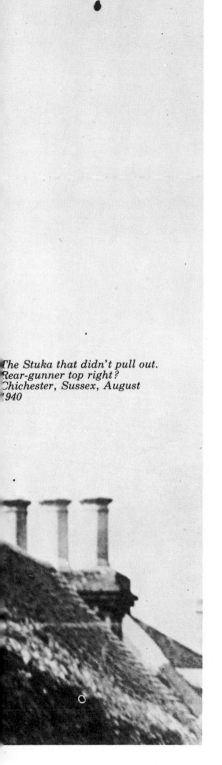

The Stuka that didn't pull out. Rear-gunner top right? Chichester, Sussex, August 1940

like a solid sheet of wind.

No sooner had he felt the parachute check his fall than he landed—bumping via a low roof into a Chelsea garden. The Dornier he had shot down spun down only a mile or so away, crashing through a shop and on to the pavement at the very entrance to Victoria Station. And some of its crew floated softly to earth right in the middle of Kennington Oval.

At this stage of the struggle it was becoming clear to the British fighter pilots that the tide was turning. The enemy bomber crews were not pressing on. As soon as our fighter pilots went into attack, and sometimes before, they were jettisoning their bombs, breaking formation, and heading for home.

Twenty Dornier 215s which were met over the London docks flying in a diamond pattern, escorted by Me 109s, stepped up to 22,000 feet. A level quarter-attack broke up the bombers, enabling intercepting fighters to pursue them towards the coast and shoot down most of them. One of them exploded in a peaceful field in south-east England to the immense surprise of a flock of sheep who were minding their own business.

In this confused fighting British squadrons sometimes found themselves outnumbering the enemy, an unusual and highly satisfactory state of affairs. On one occasion, a single Hurricane attacked twelve Me 109s. He dived underneath, shot the rear Me 109 down and then another before the enemy realized what was happening. By then he had dived away.

The first phase of the great battle of 15 September was all over by 12.30 p.m. By the time that people were ready to sit down to their Sunday lunches, the routed air armada was in full flight back to its bases in northern France. Mr Churchill had spent that day in one of the Operations rooms of 11 Group. It was seen that for once his cigar remained unlit all the time, as he followed the bewilderingly swift shifts of the battle being depicted on the table map before him.

For a fleeting moment, some of the enemy had succeeded in penetrating into the centre of the capital, but they dropped comparatively few bombs. The firing was too hot, the defence too strong. Yet despite the sound and fury of the battle, the citizens of London had their lunch in peace. As though by mutual agreement there was a lull in the conflict for about an hour and a half. It was half-time.

Then shortly after 2 p.m. fresh forces returned in about the same strength as before. Enemy aircraft crossed the coast near Dover in two waves, the first of 150, the second of 100 aircraft.

Twenty-one squadrons of Spitfires and Hurricanes attacked them. The sky was full of criss-crosses of condensation trails. The noise on the ground was like a child running a stick down the railings or that of tearing a piece of calico. Every now and then the blue was stained by the black plume of a dying aeroplane, German or British.

Left: Captured German air crew. Below: Dornier 17 and (right) Me 109—situation normal

The pilots' reports told the same story of victory:

'The whole of the nose, including the pilot's cockpit, was shot away . . .'

'I saw tracer flying past my left wing and saw a Me 109 attack me . . .'

'I saw his perspex burst and the enemy aircraft spun down . . .'

'I did not consider it worth while to waste any more ammunition upon it . . .'

'I then looked for more trouble and saw a He 111. I attacked and closed to about ten feet . . .'

'I gave him everything I had. . . .'

Winston Churchill absorbed in the Operations Room map in front of him asked Air Vice Marshal Keith Park, A.O.C. 11 Group, what fighter reserves were available. Park replied, 'There are none.' Ten minutes later the action ended. The long note of the 'all-clear' sounded level and re-assuring. The Germans had cracked. By tea-time on Sunday 15 September, the tide of the enemy offensive had been turned.

After mid-September it became obvious that the German effort was finished—although to those of us in the air it had become clearer since the beginning of September that the German pilots were not as confident as they had appeared the month before. As their morale dissipated, ours rose. We knew in our hearts it was now only a matter of time before they quit.

The enemy made one or two considerable efforts after this date, notably on 27 and 30 September. They never came again in force in daylight over London. 17 September had been Hitler's date for invasion. Our photographic reconnaissance aeroplanes had continually reported the build-up of invasion barges in the ports of northern France and Belgium. After 15 September, they noted that these were being dispersed.

This date, 15 September, is the historical Battle of Britain Day because the greatest number of enemy were shot down during it. At the time we reckoned the number was 185. After the war there was considerable argument about the numbers. The German records (or what remained of them) were dug out and the figure reduced to 56. Frankly, those of us who were present at the time disagree most emphatically with the bureaucratic acceptance of German figures which had been proved unreliable in the U-Boat campaign. My own view is that no one will know the correct assessment unless the English Channel and the Thames Estuary are drained. Anyhow nobody cares. The fact remains that the Germans quit before we did and so they lost. It's as simple as that. Thanks to Camm, Mitchell, the Hurricane, the Spitfire and every man and woman in Britain, our island kingdom was safe.

Nor should we forget the pilots themselves, the Few. The list is endless of gallant young men, many barely out of school. Some made names for themselves, some survived the war; and many

Air Vice Marshal Trafford Leigh Mallory, Commander of 12 Group

John Kilmartin   *'Ginger' Lacey*

'Sailor' Malan   *Peter Townsend*

Bob Stanford Tuck

Air Vice Marshal Keith Park, Commander of 11 Group

'Bing' Cross   'Paddy' Finucane

James Brindley Nicolson

'Cobber' Kain

did neither for they died in their first combat. I recall here some of the better known, but there are many more I could write about—as I say, the list is endless.

'Sailor' Malan had already opened his account in spectacular fashion in the sky over Dunkirk. On the night of 19 June, he destroyed two Heinkel 111s. This was the start of this superlative pilot's long and distinguished career not only as a fighter pilot but also as a leader. 74 Squadron's great record in the Battle of Britain provides ample proof of this since he commanded it throughout.

Michael Crossley started 'shooting 'em down' in France in early 1940 to continue the process as the C.O. of 32 Squadron during the Battle. One of his pilots of that period told me a remarkable story about Mike. He shot a Ju 87 dive bomber at the top of its zoom having released its bomb; as it collapsed from his burst the Ju 87 behind collided with it; followed by number three hitting the first two; so Mike got three enemy aircraft with a single burst. I last saw him in Rhodesia in 1965, looking much the same as in his heyday.

Other names becoming famous in the Battle, all of whom are alive and kicking today, were Colin Grey (from New Zealand), Ginger Lacey, and Don Kingaby.

Then there was Bob Stanford Tuck. I first met him in May 1940 on Martlesham airfield when we were both Flight Lieutenants in different Spitfire squadrons and about to see our first action over Dunkirk. He looked like a matador and subsequently proved to be a pretty good one in the air. Strangely he nearly failed his flying course when he joined the Royal Air Force a year or two before the war. He was a fine shot, and this I think was the main reason for his great successes at Dunkirk, during the Battle of Britain, and in the subsequent operations over northern France in 1941. Like many, Bob had his lucky escapes but undoubtedly the most fortunate one was early in 1941. He was drinking with some chums in a local pub in Norfolk and decided to leave early. No one else would come with him. A matter of minutes after he left, the pub was hit by an enemy bomb and everyone inside was killed. He was a prisoner of war from 1942 until the end and now farms in Kent, looking exactly the same as when we first met in 1940.

Two names that were household words during that high summer of 1940 were John Mungo Park and H. M. ('Steve') Stephen, both of 74 Squadron. Their names were then always coupled and appropriately they shared the destruction of a Me 109 on 30 November 1940, to bring Biggin Hill fighter station its 600th victory. This figure was the combined total of victories of all the squadrons which had operated from Biggin. A notable achievement. Stephen survived the War and is now the Managing Director of the *Daily Telegraph*; Mungo Park died in his Spitfire over France on 17 June, 1941.

6TH HURRICAN SQ

Battle for the Mediterranean

Malta under attack. The island was defended by Hurricanes—with spectacular help from 'Faith' (inset), 'Hope', and 'Charity'—the three magnificent but antiquated Gloster Gladiators

MALTA

Far away from the war-torn south of England, another battle was being waged. Not on such a grand scale, but for very high stakes, the control of the Mediterranean, of which Malta was the key. From June 1940 to November 1942, the island had 3,215 air-raid warnings: an average of one every seven hours for two and a half years. The enemy dropped 14,000 tons of bombs, killed 1,468 civilians, destroyed or damaged 24,000 buildings, and lost 1,129 aircraft.

When the battle began on 10 June 1940, the date Italy entered the war, the defence of Malta rested on three Gladiators which became known as *Faith*, *Hope*, and *Charity*. For three weeks, quite incredibly this trio took on the full weight of the Italian air force sent to crush the island.

At the end of June, however, four Hurricanes arrived and throughout July these seven fighters alone faced about two hundred enemy aircraft operating from Sicily. Raids were carried out almost every day. The defence was so fierce that eventually the Italians—despite their enormous superiority in numbers—only ventured over the island by night. The British losses were one Hurricane and one Gladiator.

On 2 August 1940, H.M.S. *Argus* steamed to within 200 miles of Malta to fly off twelve Hurricanes and two Skuas. This consignment arrived safely and formed the basis for a more effective fighter defence. During August the enemy turned from the dockyards to the airfields, attempting to smash Malta's first line of defence. Then the Italians brought in German dive-bombers, Junkers 87s. Twenty of these attacked Hal Far airfield on 15 September, dropping delayed-action bombs.

But it was the arrival of the Luftwaffe on Sicilian airfields that marked a grimmer stage in the long battle.

On 17 November, twelve more Hurricanes were embarked on H.M.S. *Argus*. The Italian fleet forced the carrier to put about

at the Hurricanes' extreme range from Malta. Out of twelve Hurricanes and two Skuas, only four Hurricanes and one Skua reached Luqa, Malta. The rest ran out of fuel. A costly error.

Soon afterwards, the aircraft carrier H.M.S. *Illustrious* steamed into Grand Harbour with a convoy. She was listing and badly down by the stern, having been dive-bombed by the Germans for seven hours. During the next few hours, the sirens sounded for enemy reconnaissance planes several times. The people waited for the inevitable attack: Hurricanes and naval Fulmar fighters waited as well.

The plan to defend the *Illustrious* was to put up a fierce anti-aircraft barrage, creating a curtain of fire over the harbour. The dive-bombers would have to fly through this to reach their targets. Between 13.00 hours and 14.45 over seventy aircraft came in.

As the barrage began, Malta had never heard such a noise, and it was amplified by the guns of the ships in the harbour. The fighters waited to catch the enemy as they came in and then later as they banked away from Grand Harbour. Sometimes the fighters followed the enemy in through the barrage. Two hundred houses were wiped out by the raid and five hundred damaged. The church clock of Our Lady of Victories pointed to twenty past two for the rest of the war, a reminder of that fierce afternoon of 16 January 1941. But the carrier *Illustrious* was still there.

Two days later, eighty dive-bombers attacked the airfields at Luqa and Hal Far in an attempt to engage and reduce the number of fighters defending the *Illustrious*. For a time, Luqa went out of action. The island's striking forces became badly depleted, but Malta's own few pilots shot down seven of the enemy aircraft, while four more went to ground-gunners.

Next day, 19 January, the Germans again attacked the Grand Harbour. Six Hurricanes, one Fulmar and a Gladiator met them. The fighters shot down eleven, the guns eight, and the surviving three-quarters of the raiders retreated. On 23 January, the *Illustrious* escaped, sailing east under her own power. Two days later she was safe in Alexandria.

In February 1941 began the second German assault from the air. The enemy made large-scale minelaying raids on the harbours and creeks. On 17 February, the island had raids for the eleventh night in succession, yet the harbour remained effective.

The pilots of the small Hurricane force were losing a lot of sleep, but still having to face the sweeps of Me 109s. On 16 February, two enemy formations came over Malta. The Me 109s split up on sighting the Hurricanes, one formation climbing above, the other dropping below. Flight Lieutenant J. A. F. MacLachlan led a Hurricane flight and described his experience:

'While on patrol over Luqa at 20,000 feet, we were attacked from above and astern by six Me 109s. As previously arranged,

Top: HMS Illustrious *enters the Grand Harbour at Malta.*

Bottom: Illustrious *under attack*

the flight broke away to the right and formed a defensive circle. As I took my place in the circle, I saw four more Me 109s coming out of the sun. Just as they came within range, I turned back towards them and they all overshot me without firing. I looked very carefully but could see no more enemy aircraft above me, so I turned back to the tail of the nearest 109. I was turning well inside him and was just about to open fire when I was hit in the left arm by a cannon shell. My dashboard was completely smashed so I baled out and landed safely by parachute.'

MacLachlan's left arm was amputated at Imtarfa Hospital. When he came out, a colleague flew him round in a Magister. Then he took off by himself and landed faultlessly. A few days later, he flew a Hurricane and asked to rejoin his squadron. Back in Britain he had an artificial arm fitted and flew on many more successful operations.

The statistics of the battle were sensational. Since the out-break of war, the few fighters on Malta had claimed as many as ninety-six aircraft destroyed for the loss of sixteen fighters and eleven pilots. But the enemy were slowly gaining an upper hand and flying lower and lower. They were neutralizing the striking power of the air defence, and in the course of ten days nearly all the R.A.F. flight leaders were lost. At the beginning of March 1941 an official signal reported:

'Blitz raid of several formations totalling certainly no less than 100 aircraft, of which at least 60 bombers, attacked Hal Far. A few of these aircraft dropped bombs and machine-gunned Kala-franca. Damage at Kalafranca was slight both to buildings and aircraft. One Sunderland unserviceable for a few days. Damage Hal Far still being assessed.

'Preliminary report as follows: three Swordfish and one Gladiator burnt out. All other aircraft temporarily unserviceable All barrack blocks unserviceable and one demolished. Water and power cut off. Hangars considerably damaged. Airfield temporarily unserviceable. Eleven fighters up. Enemy casualties by our fighters, two Ju 88s, two Ju 87s, one Do 215, two Me 109s, confirmed. One Ju 88 and three Ju 87s damaged. By AA, one Me 110 and eight other aircraft confirmed, also four damaged. There are probably others which did not reach their base but cannot be checked. One Hurricane and one pilot lost after first shooting down one Ju 87 included above.

'For the blitz every serviceable Hurricane and every available pilot was put up and they achieved results against extremely heavy odds. The only answer to this kind of thing is obviously more fighters and these must somehow be provided if the air defence of Malta is to be maintained.'

The raids did not decrease, but towards the end of April another twenty-three Hurricanes arrived. A month later, more Hurricanes flew in—and about June the Luftwaffe left Sicily for the Russian front. Even so, the battle for Malta was not yet over.

7 BALKAN BLITZKRIEG
Hopeless odds

While Malta was struggling to survive the first round of her air/sea battle, the Axis powers struck into the Balkans. Italy went for Greece via Albania; then Germany invaded Bulgaria.

As an emergency measure, Gladiator squadrons 33, 80, and 112 were ordered to Greece, but it was soon realized that Hurricanes were what was really required. The initial consignment got to Greece on 7 February 1941, to be commanded by Flight Lieutenant 'Pat' Pattle, a South African who had already scored early successes in the Middle East.

On 28 February—the day before the Germans moved into Bulgaria—twenty-eight fighters, sixteen Hurricanes and twelve Gladiators, met a large force of Fiats. In an hour and a half they accounted for twenty-seven of the enemy, half of their total force. Pat Pattle got five of them. After his first two, he had to fly back to Paramythia to refuel and rearm; then he hurried back

into the same battle to wipe out another three Fiats near Valona.

Five weeks later, on 6 April, the Germans attacked Yugoslavia. Fortunately, Hurricanes had at that stage superseded virtually all of the Gladiators in Greece. The enemy possessed a vast numerical advantage of aircraft near the fighting areas, so the decision had to be made, reluctantly, to group the Hurricane squadrons in the Athens region. Within a fortnight, by 19 April, the four squadrons of Hurricanes could count on only twenty-two serviceable aircraft instead of forty-eight. Yet they managed to intercept three separate raids on that date, scoring eight victories while sustaining damage to three Hurricanes.

The next day about one hundred enemy aircraft mounted a major air attack on Piraeus, the port of Athens. Junkers 88s, Me 109s and 110s filled the skies over the port. Pattle had just fifteen Hurricanes at his disposal. He led a dozen to tackle the fighters, the other three of them going for the dive-bombers. Fourteen enemy aircraft were destroyed against five precious Hurricanes. Pattle himself shot down three enemy fighters before veering off to help another Hurricane pilot. Two Me 109s shot him down into the sea off Megara.

This was a serious blow to the remainder of the Hurricane pilots, whose own days in Greece were now clearly numbered. The next orders, dated 22–23 April, told all remaining British aeroplanes—other than the few Hurricanes—to withdraw either to Crete or Egypt. The final act of the air campaign came soon afterwards, when a force of Me 110s attacked the Hurricanes dispersed on the airfield at Argos. After the raid, seven Hurricanes were left. These were sent to Crete.

The story of Crete was much the same, with our fighters taking on overwhelming odds in the air. For the first fortnight of May, Crete received regular air attacks as a softening up for a forthcoming invasion. The defending aircraft were Fulmars, Gladiators, and Hurricanes, all continually in action. The enemy caught the Fulmars on the ground one day, which left a dozen Hurricanes and three Gladiators.

Twelve more Hurricanes were flown from Egypt to Heraklion airfield, but in the confusion that now reigned, our naval forces shot down two and prevented four more from landing there. As a result only four Hurricanes got through to Heraklion. These were destroyed on the ground by enemy action.

Nevertheless, the statistics were inspiring. In the seventeen days around the period of the invasion of Crete, three Hurricane squadrons claimed about 125 enemy aircraft for the loss in action of twenty-eight Hurricanes and sixteen pilots. A mere handful got away as the island fell.

German airman poses in captured British aeroplane at Greek aerodrome. He is wearing a Serbian headdress doubtless acquired on his way through Yugoslavia

8 ATTACK & DEFENCE
From the Mersey to Murmansk

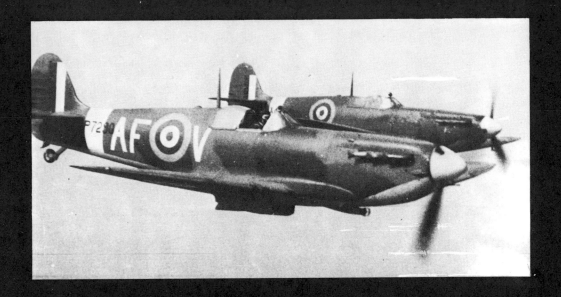

Back in Britain during the winter of 1940–41, the German bomber Blitz was at its height. Night after night the bombers droned overhead creating an inferno below.

London burns in the Blitz. Inset: spearhead of fighter offensive, Spitfire Mark IIa

Specially equipped night-fighters with trained crews had not been developed by the end of 1940, so it was decided that Hurricanes and Spitfires would be sent up on clear nights to destroy enemy bombers. Not many fighter pilots had night-flying experience. With the lull after the heavy fighting during the Battle of Britain, all were keen to have a go. Successes were few and far between because it was sheer luck for a Spitfire or Hurricane pilot to see another aeroplane in the dark. The pilot was sitting behind a twelve-cylinder engine; on each side of the long nose in front of his windscreen were six short exhaust stubs which spouted flame thereby eliminating forward visibility.

In November the first heavy raid on Coventry took place. It was a clear night with a full moon. Three of us in 242 Squadron took off eagerly from Duxford in our Hurricanes with instructions to patrol the target area from 13,000 feet upwards; we were to be stepped up at 1,000 feet intervals. We were restricted to heights above 12,000 feet to avoid anti-aircraft fire. None of us saw a thing except fires and gun flashes below. A few months later, I had exactly the same experience over Portsmouth in a Spitfire from Tangmere. Same instructions, same weather, same result.

Night interception was a highly specialized technique, but success abounded with the advent of the Beaufighter, and subsequently the Mosquito, twin-engined and radar-equipped with a crew of two and four 20-mm. cannons. Exceptional pilots like John Cunningham (our most famous post-war test pilot), Bob Braham, Tom Pike (later to become Chief of Air Staff), Rory Chisholm (after the war a senior executive with British Petroleum), and others were brilliantly successful at this night interception business.

Of the few successes by Hurricane and Spitfire pilots, one must be recorded. Sergeant MacNair took off in his Hurricane of 96 Squadron at 20.30 hours one evening with instructions to patrol the Liverpool area. In bright moonlight, he could see the fires started by the enemy bombers very clearly. Suddenly he also spotted a Heinkel 111k heading south. He was in fact flying north-east at that moment, but at once turned towards the bomber. He got to seventy-five yards behind its tail, and with his sight trained on its dark silhouette, he opened fire twice for four seconds. The windscreen of the Hurricane became smothered in oil. He veered away and noticed that the port engine of the Heinkel was giving off volumes of smoke. At the same sort of range, MacNair made another attempt, again scoring hits with a four-second burst. By now the Heinkel was getting lower by the second and going out of control. He used the rest of his ammunition on a beam attack from port, sending the bomber crashing down somewhere near the Mersey and Widnes. By that stage MacNair was at an altitude of only 3,500 feet—dangerously near to the balloon barrage—so he gained height quickly and carefully. The total flight time was two hours and forty minutes, and by the time he touched down at Cranage he had virtually no fuel left.

Fighter Command went on the offensive at the end of 1940. As an opening gambit, two Spitfires from 66 Squadron, Biggin Hill, shot up Le Touquet airfield on 20 December. On 9 January 1941 five squadrons ventured thirty miles inland beyond the French coast. Next day, Spitfires and Hurricanes of six squadrons gave fighter protection to a force of Blenheims attacking enemy aircraft on an airfield in the Calais region. We lost a Hurricane, and a couple of Spitfires crash-landed on their return to England.

In March 1941 I was posted to Tangmere, Sussex, as wing leader of what soon became known as the Tangmere Wing. Johnnie Johnson, the top scoring British pilot of World War II, flew with me at that time and he has described the type of formation flying which was developed at Tangmere: 'Tactically, because the enemy abreast formation was better than the astern pattern, Fighter Command lagged behind the German Fighter Arm. It was not until this spring that Douglas Bader copied the Schwarme, which he called the "finger-four" because the relative positions of the fighters are similar to a plan view of one's outstretched fingertips. Bader's pilots were immediately

Spitfire IIs at Kirton-in-Lindsey

impressed with their finger-fours, for, unlike the line astern pattern, all pilots were always covered, and all stood an equal chance of survival. Soon all fighter squadrons followed Bader's lead. It had taken a long time to relearn the doctrine of Oswald Boelcke [the German World War I ace].'

Laddie Lucas, another distinguished fighter pilot, has said:

'As I see it, every pilot in the R.A.F. owed something to what went on in World War I. These tactics were used again, by ourselves and by the Germans. But the actual line abreast flying, the basic concept of a pair of aircraft, or four aeroplanes in the form of a finger-four formation—these were fundamental tactics whether used in World War I, by the Spaniards, or the Germans, or whoever else. The fact of it was that Douglas modernized it, brought it up to date, made it fresh and practical for flying in the 1940s. And don't forget this was in direct conflict with a lot of the flying thinking that was being done in 11 Group, which was all line astern. It was quite all right to climb a squadron on a wing in line astern to battle height, but then so often they stayed together like that and never came up to line abreast. Terrible for the junior pilots as ass-end Charlie! Douglas started with the basic two aeroplanes, then the finger-four, then the fours in touch with each other, one squadron, two squadrons, and three squadrons. This was the basis, with two pilots looking inwards, so that the whole sky was covered right through 180 degrees. This was really fundamental to all his flying, both

defensively and offensively in the sweeps over the north of France from Tangmere. Douglas never claimed to have pioneered the technique.'

Hugh 'Cocky' Dundas, yet another of the 'greats', has added:

'Douglas was very much a pioneer in getting away from that line astern formation. In fact he and I conducted an experiment together, following a long conversation in the mess. We tried a bit of finger-four and adopted it. I certainly never flew anything else for the rest of the war. We were flying over France all the time now, instead of over England. We were doing sweep after sweep after sweep, all day, every day. We always flew in fours. I flew as the other leader, next to him. We did over sixty sweeps together that summer before he crashed.'

Cocky Dundas and I never claimed to have invented the formula, we just adapted it to the current conditions. Other changes at that time were the advance from the Spitfire Mk 1 to Mk II, matched by the enemy's Messerschmitt Me 109f, followed quickly by the Mk Vb.

Apart from the Tangmere Wing, there were now Spitfire Wings at Biggin Hill and Hornchurch; Spitfire/Hurricane Wings at Duxford, Middle Wallop and Wittering; Hurricane Wings at Kenley, Northolt and North Weald.

Now that we were on the offensive, our formula was different from that of the Germans. The Air Staff had digested the mistakes made by the Luftwaffe in the Battle of Britain. Instead of going over with masses of bombers and fighters, we conducted our attacks with a small number of bombers and a lot of fighters. Our intention was to hit specific targets in France and not—as the Germans did—bomb indiscriminately, and kill a lot of civilians. The bombing force usually consisted of four Lancasters or Halifaxes (four-engined heavy bombers which carried a big load on these short missions) or a squadron of Blenheims.

The method was as follows: the bombers would fly down from their base in Lincolnshire or Yorkshire, rendezvous with the close-support wing (thirty-six Hurricanes or Spitfires) over the fighter base. The bombers' favourite height was 12,000 feet, and the fighters would virtually envelop them from that height upwards. This formation would then be joined by the close-escort wing (thirty-six Spitfires) which built up the formation to around 20,000 feet.

It looked like a large bee-hive moving across the sky. In fact someone christened it 'the bee-hive', and the name crept into official correspondence and signals. While this mass was flying across the Channel towards France, target support wings would take off from south-east aerodromes at heights between 20,000 and 30,000 feet, timed to arrive in the target area with the bee-hive. Their objective was to destroy enemy fighters on their way to attack the bee-hive. A further refinement was the introduction of a target-withdrawal wing which arrived over the

The Blitz: woman rescued from bombed house and Londoners sheltering in Underground

target area as the bee-hive and all the rest of us turned for home. These chaps were full of ammunition and happy to clean up any mess that was going.

It was all done to precise timing and worked like clockwork. During the whole of the summer of 1941 hardly a bomber was lost on these operations.

The object of these offensive sorties over France was three-fold—to destroy factories working for the Germans; to destroy German fighters; to compel the German High Command to keep units of the Luftwaffe in France instead of sending them to the Russian front. Additionally it was good for the morale of our occupied French allies to see the Royal Air Force over France.

It was on one of these raids, on 9 August 1941, that my Spitfire collided in mid-air with a Me 109. I did not fly again for nearly four years. . . .

Allied air and ground crews began to be formed into fighter squadrons: on 17 November 1941 the Belgian 350 Squadron was formed, to be followed by a second one, 349 Squadron. There were eight Free French squadrons altogether, the first of the several Spitfire squadrons dating from 7 November 1941. Dutch, Czechs, Poles and Norwegians all had Spitfire squadrons too.

Britain was determined to help Russia, now reeling under the heavy and successful onslaught of the German armies thrusting along a 1,500 mile front for Leningrad, Moscow, and the oil-fields in the south. The only way we could help was by sending supplies by sea via the far northern ports of Russia. But since the neighbouring nation of Finland was on Germany's side, the Russian ports were within reach of enemy air attack.

An early decision was made for Hurricanes to be transported to Russia as air defence against enemy attacks on the forth-coming convoys at their ports of destination. Wing Commander H. N. G. Ramsbottom Isherwood, a notable New Zealander, formed a two-squadron Wing—Nos. 81 and 134—at Leconfield as early as 12 August 1941, just six weeks after the German invasion. The squadrons were equipped with Hurricane Mk IIbs (twelve machine guns); two dozen were shipped on H.M.S. *Argus* and a further fifteen in crates via merchant ships in a convoy under preparation. Some of the personnel sailed in the *Argus*, the rest with their crated aircraft in the convoy. By 28 August the carrier was safely off Murmansk, and the twenty-four Hurricanes flew off to land at Vaenga. As if to demonstrate the need for the fighters, enemy air attacks forced the rest of the contingent to change course for Archangel. The Wing was thus in two parts, with twenty-four Hurricanes and their pilots at Vaenga and all the ground crew with the crated aircraft at Archangel. Eventually they were reunited.

Five of 81 Squadron Hurricanes encountered the Luftwaffe on the following day and they destroyed three out of five Messer-schmitts.

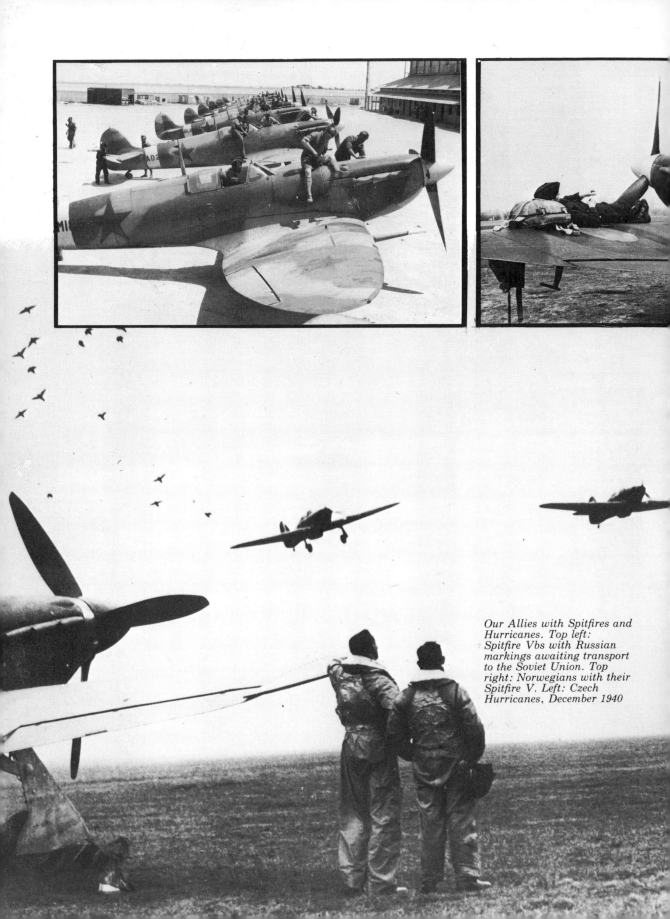

Our Allies with Spitfires and Hurricanes. Top left: Spitfire Vbs with Russian markings awaiting transport to the Soviet Union. Top right: Norwegians with their Spitfire V. Left: Czech Hurricanes, December 1940

e story of the Battle of Britain
ild not be complete without
erence to the Czech and Polish
adrons which fought alongside us
ighter Command at that time.
ie Czech and Polish military
ots had escaped from their
upied countries in 1938 and 1939,
I made their way through
nce to England. All were
erienced fliers united in hatred
he common foe. Polish
rricane) squadrons were 302 and
; Czech (Hurricane), 310 and 312.
that time all had British
adron commanders. 302 (S/Ldr
chell) and 310 (S/Ldr Blackwood)
ied the Duxford Wing in
tember during the height of the
tle. Polish 303 Squadron was
bably the most famous of all
ed squadrons with Fighter
mand. Rugged, tough,
icated fighters, they were led by
dr R. G. Kellett. Small of stature,
h a round cherubic face and
en hair, his looks belied him.
had the heart of a lion and was
rugged and relentless as any of
se he led. In 1940, 303 was based
Northolt which was commanded
(World War I) Group Captain
nley Vincent. He would slip into
oare Hurricane on occasion and
oattle with the enemy. A great
ce Northolt in 1940. The Polish
r Memorial stands at one corner
he airfield to this day to remind
not only of those brave pilots of
Squadron but of all their
apatriots who followed during the
t five years, fourteen squadrons
ll. Names like Urbanowicz,
lski, Janus ring the bell of fame.

Four days later, orders were received by the Hurricanes to protect a force of Russian bombers returning from a raid. They turned out to be eight Me 109s. The eight Hurricanes destroyed two Me 109s. Then on 26 September, 81 Squadron were jumped while escorting Russian bombers. The Hurricanes outmanoeuvred the enemy and accounted for three Me 109fs.

The record by the close of September stood at twelve successes against one pilot lost by 81 Squadron, and four successes without loss by 134 Squadron. That pilot was the only one killed throughout this Russian episode. With October came a decline in enemy attention to the area. The Royal Air Force pilots trained their Russian counterparts to handle the Hurricanes, and by the end of 1941 their role was ended. It was, however, the beginning of the thousands of Allied aircraft accepted by the Russians.

Towards the end of 1941 the Hurricane Mk IIc appeared. In addition to a more powerful Merlin engine, it had the heavy armament of four 20-mm cannons. This really was something, not for fighter versus fighter combat, but for all sorts of low-level roles and for night intruder sorties. Later, the Hurricane wing was strengthened to take a 40-mm calibre gun. The Mk IId carried two of these plus fifteen rounds of ammunition for each. Rockets and bombs also became part of the armament of Spitfire and Hurricane—with the invasion of Europe and close Army support in mind.

The Spitfire Mk Vb (two cannons and four machine guns) with a more powerful engine appeared in the early summer of 1941. This was a notable improvement over the Mk II. When we got these at Tangmere in 1941, we were entirely happy against the latest Me 109f. These two aeroplanes were just about equal, with the Spitfire being stronger and of course able to turn inside its rival. Then came the lean period when the Focke-Wulf 190 outflew the Spitfire Vb in every respect, before the Spitfire IXb arrived to redress the balance. Al Deere describes the IXb as 'a prince among princes, a champion among champions, perhaps the greatest fighter in its era of all time'. It possessed all the earlier tried and tested qualities of its predecessors but its Merlin 66 engine, with a rated altitude of 21,000 feet, gave it a 30 m.p.h. advantage over the FW 190 at that height; and this coupled with its astounding rate of climb, meant that for the remainder of the war the Spitfire winged supreme over the war-torn skies of Europe.

On 12 February 1942, two Spitfire pilots Group Captain Victor Beamish and Wing Commander Adrian Boyd caught sight of the three German warships *Scharnhorst*, *Gneisenau* and *Prinz Eugen* in the English Channel. Six Swordfish of the Fleet Air Arm made an attempt to attack by torpedo in the face of the ships' guns and also the new Focke-Wulf 190 fighters. Spitfires had the job of top cover for the Swordfish, against the Focke-

Wulfs. Three squadrons took off from Biggin Hill, while the Hornchurch Wing (Spitfires) were to give close support. Ten Spitfires of the latter force managed to keep in touch with the Swordfish and broke up a Me 109 force which also appeared. But nothing could prevent the Swordfish being destroyed by the barrage from the three ships.

The leader of the Swordfish formation, Lieutenant Commander Eugene Esmonde, was posthumously awarded the V.C.

One of the new names of this phase of the war was the Dublin-born Brendan 'Paddy' Finucane. Between the beginning of August 1941 and the end of October, he destroyed eighteen Me 109s. After further victories he became Wing Commander on 27 June 1942. On 15 July 1942, he was shot down into the Channel and killed.

On 19 August 1942, Operation Jubilee, the ill-conceived Dieppe raid, took place. Spitfires of 129 Squadron flew over the port at dawn. They were followed by high-level Spitfire patrols to operate as the fighter umbrella for Blenheims, Bostons, and the new 'Hurribombers' which were to go for the five Dieppe gun batteries. Hurribombers were Hurricane Mk IIbs adapted for fighter-bomber role by the mounting of two 250-lb bombs underneath. At first the enemy air resistance was sluggish, but it grew stiffer by midday. Four squadrons of Spitfires kept the sky clear, while four more Spitfire squadrons escorted twenty-four Flying Fortress bombers attacking the Abbeville airfield in an effort to reduce enemy air activity.

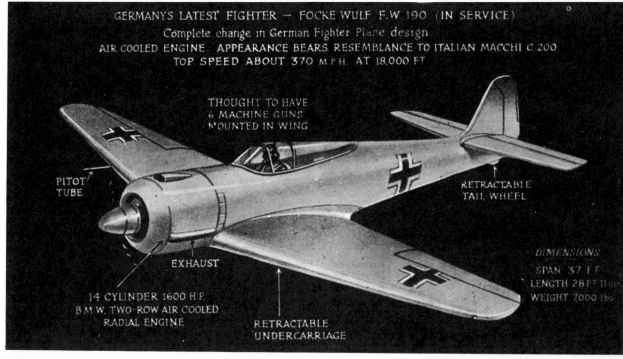

GERMANY'S LATEST FIGHTER — FOCKE WULF F.W. 190 (IN SERVICE)
Complete change in German Fighter Plane design
AIR COOLED ENGINE. APPEARANCE BEARS RESEMBLANCE TO ITALIAN MACCHI C 200
TOP SPEED ABOUT 370 M.P.H. AT 18,000 FT

THOUGHT TO HAVE
6 MACHINE GUNS
MOUNTED IN WING

PITOT
TUBE

RETRACTABLE
TAIL WHEEL

EXHAUST

DIMENSIONS
SPAN 37 FT
LENGTH 28 FT 11 ins.
WEIGHT 7000 lbs

14 CYLINDER 1600 H.P.
B.M.W. TWO-ROW AIR COOLED
RADIAL ENGINE

RETRACTABLE
UNDERCARRIAGE

Top: 'Hurribomber'—Hurricane IIb adapted for fighter-bomber role with two 250-lb bombs underneath

Below right: Hurricane Mark IIc—with four 20-mm cannons, formidable in low-level roles and night intruder sorties

Below left: wartime illustration of the Focke-Wulf 190

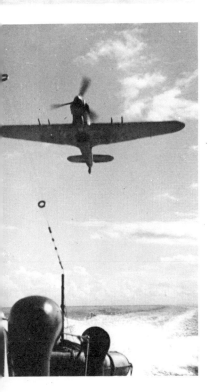

More air sorties were made this day than on any other during the war so far. Of the forty-eight Spitfire squadrons engaged, all but six were equipped with the latest Mk IXb. The air fighting proved successful, though the raid itself was a disaster.

The Hurribombers were later to prove themselves elsewhere. Their advantage was that they flew practically at ground-level, or sea-level, and could drop their bombs in flight with greater accuracy than could generally be achieved in dive-bombing. Here is one version of a Hurribomber operation over Europe:

'The impression and thrill of speed near the ground has to be experienced to be believed. Our bombs are fitted with delayed-action fuses, so that they do not explode until we have got well outside their blast range. It might seem that, flying on to the target at only a few feet altitude, we would be easy prey. We would be if the gunners could see us coming. But generally they cannot see the low-flying fighter until it is almost overhead, and then they have to be remarkably quick to get the gun trained on the fleeting aircraft. Moreover, they have little time to calculate what deflections to allow in their aim. On the other hand, of course, the pilot would have precious little chance of baling out if his aircraft were hit. So far, however, the advantage seems to be on our side. I have seen flak and machine-gun fire pelting at my aircraft from all angles, but none of it has hit me. We get intimate, if lightning, pictures of the countryside. People on the road, soldiers scrambling for cover, bombs bursting and throwing up debris around us.

'Our first big day recently was typical of the work of this new weapon of ours. We went over in half a gale. The target we were looking for eluded us on this particular occasion. I think we passed it only a mile to one side. We did a circuit and not seeing our main target, began to look for an alternative.

'I found myself flying down a river with a main line railway running alongside. Ahead was a bridge, carrying the railway over the river. I called to my companion that I would bomb the bridge, and together we swept over it, barely skimming the structure, and let our bombs go. Another pair in the squadron coming on behind us saw the bombs explode in the river and the whole bridge slump to one side. As they passed over it, they saw the bridge looking as crooked as an eel.

'I looked back to see the effect of our bombs, but all I saw was a string of tracer bullets going up behind my port wing. As I turned again, I saw it was coming from a gun-post on an aerodrome which my companion and I were already traversing. I was halfway across it before I recognized it as an aerodrome, but I was in time to give some huts on the far edge a burst from my guns. After this I made for the coast again, flying slap over a town and straight down one of its main streets! The squadron reassembled just off the coast, and we beat it back to our base. We sustained no damage at all.'

Duel with the Focke-Wulf by 'Johnnie' Johnson

I never encountered these formidable fighters at first hand. Air Vice Marshal 'Johnnie' Johnson (then Squadron Leader and later Wing Commander) certainly did. Here are some of his experiences of the 'brutes' (as he calls them).

The Focke-Wulf 190 was undoubtedly the best German fighter. We had first seen it in late 1941. We were puzzled by the unfamiliar silhouette, for these new German fighters seemed to have squarer wingtips and more tapering fuselages than the Messerschmitts we usually encountered. We saw that the new aircraft had radial engines and a mixed armament of cannons and machine guns, all firing from wing positions.

Whatever these strange fighters were, they gave us a hard time of it. They seemed to be faster in a zoom climb than the Me 109, and far more stable in a vertical dive. They also turned better. The first time we saw them we all had our work cut out to shake them off, and we lost several pilots.

Back at our fighter base and encouraged by our enthusiastic Intelligence Officer, we drew sketches and side views of this strange new aeroplane. We were all agreed that it was superior to the Me 109f and completely outclassed our Spitfire Vs. Our sketches disappeared into mysterious Intelligence channels and we heard no more of the matter. But from then on, fighter pilots continually reported increasing numbers of these outstanding fighters over northern France.

Later, we were given the novel explanation that the new enemy fighters were probably some batch of Curtis Hawk aeroplanes which the French had bought from the United States shortly before the war. It was suggested to us that the Luftwaffe had taken over the Curtis Hawks and were using them operationally. This was a ridiculous theory, for no pre-war aircraft had a performance to compare with these brutes. It was not until 1942 that our intelligence admitted the introduction of a completely new German fighter, the redoubtable Focke-Wulf 190.

In August 1942 I had my first duel with a 190.

I was leading the Auxiliary 610 Squadron (County of Chester), flying over Canadian troops who were taking part in the disastrous combined operation against Dieppe. At 10,000 feet my squadron had been badly 'bounced' by a large number of 109s and 190s. In the ensuing dog-fight I got in a long burst at a 190 which began to smoke; the wheels dropped and it fell away towards the sea. Immediately afterwards, another large bunch of enemy aircraft came down on us from astern and the flanks. In the ensuing dog-fight the squadron became split up and I found myself alone in a hostile sky. The only thing to do was to get out as quickly as possible—the golden rule in those days was that there was no future in flying alone. But as I was making my way towards the coast, I spotted a solitary aircraft over the town. I eased towards it and recognized the enemy fighter as a 190. I yawed my Spitfire to cover the blind spot behind me and to make certain that I was not about to be attacked. These movements attracted the attention of the enemy pilot. He snaked towards me almost head on. Then we both turned hard to the left and whirled round on opposite sides of what seemed to be an ever decreasing circle.

'Johnnie' Johnson

With wide-open throttles I held the Spitfire V in the tightest of vertical turns. I was greying out. Where was this German, who should, according to my reckoning, be filling the gunsight? I could not see him, and little wonder, for he was gaining on me—in another couple of turns he would have me in his sights. My over-confidence of a few seconds before had already given way to irritation at losing my opponent. This was in turn replaced by a sickening apprehension as the 190 gained on my tail. I asked the Spitfire for all she had in the turn, but the enemy pilot hung behind like a leech—it could only be a question of time . . .

Stick over and well forward, I plunged into a near vertical dive. A dangerous manoeuvre, for the 190 was more stable and faster than my Spitfire at this sort of game. But I had decided on a possible means of escape. At ground level I pulled into another steep turn, and as I gauged the height and watched the rooftops flash by I caught a glimpse of the Dieppe promenade. Of stationary tanks. Of the white casino and a deserted beach. But I had no time to admire the view. The 190 was still behind.

A short distance off-shore I could see one of our destroyers surrounded by a clutter of smaller ships. We had been carefully briefed not to fly below 4,000 feet over these destroyers —otherwise they would open fire at either friend or foe. I rammed the throttle into the emergency position, broke off my turn, and— at sea level—headed straight for the destroyer. Flak and tracer came straight at me from the destroyer, and more, slower tracer from the 190 behind passed over the top of the cockpit. At the last moment I pulled over the mast of the destroyer, then slammed the nose down hard and eased out a few feet above the sea. I broke hard to the left and searched for the 190. He was no longer with me. Either the flak from the destroyer had put him off or, better still, had shot him down. I made off at high speed for our own south coast.

During the summer of 1942 I had lost to the 190s quite a number of fighter pilots from 610 Squadron. They had given us a hard time. They were so superior to our Spitfire Vs that our excursions into France and the Low Countries had to be severely curtailed. In the summer of 1943 I was appointed wing leader of the Canadian fighter wing at Kenley. Here we had the latest in the long line of Spitfires, the redoubtable Spitfire IX. It had a bigger and far more powerful engine than that of the Spitfire V. We had heard that the Spitfire IX was superior to the 190. Now, at long last, I had the opportunity to prove it. After the long time on the inferior Spitfire V, I can only describe the move to Kenley as moving from the third division into the first division. A few days later I first flew my new Spitfire IX against the 190s. Leading the Kenley Wing and following the instructions of an excellent radar controller, we 'bounced' twenty or so 190s and shot down six for the loss of one of my Canadian fighter pilots.

Throughout that summer of 1943, we struck hard at the 190s. When they did not react to our fighter sweeps, our Typhoons dive-bombed their airfields and flushed them into the air, where we were ready and waiting and smacked them down with our superior IXs. That summer the Canadian Wing at Kenley and the Spitfire IX redressed the balance. We enjoyed doing it.

Denys Gillam— 'unrivalled maestro of the low-level attack'

Denys Gillam—then and now

Denys Gillam joined the Royal Air Force before the start of the war. He came from Yorkshire. When the war started, he was one of the three regular officers in the Auxiliary 616 Squadron (Spitfires), based at Leconfield, Yorkshire. Towards the end of May it was moved to Southend to cover the Dunkirk evacuation. Afterwards it returned to Leconfield whence on August 15 it had a splendidly successful victory over a formation of Ju 88s which were intercepted off the Yorkshire coast. Eight of the enemy were destroyed and others damaged without loss. Fortunately the two flights of 616 were in the process of changing over the 'readiness' duty when the alarm went, so the whole squadron took off after the enemy. On August 19 the squadron went to Kenley, Surrey, with their full complement of Spitfires (eighteen) and twenty-two pilots. In a few days of action they required eight new pilots and twelve Spitfires. On September 3 the squadron was withdrawn. Three fit pilots remained.

After the Battle of Britain, Gillam was posted to command 312 Czech Squadron (Hurricanes) at Speke (Liverpool). On October 8, what I believe to be the quickest recorded destruction of an enemy took place. Gillam, taking off in his Hurricane from Speke, was scarcely off the ground when he saw a Ju 88 on a low-level sortie flying straight towards him under the cloud. The 88 started turning left and climbing for the low cloud. Gillam turned right, fired a short deflection burst, then another from behind. A puff of black smoke came from the

Junkers and it landed on the mud bank of the estuary which flows past Speke. Gillam landed back on the airfield. The period from take-off to landing had occupied less than ten minutes.

On September 12, 1941, Gillam took over 615 Squadron at Manston. This was equipped with the Hurricane IIc which mounted four 20-mm cannons, two in each wing. It was a formidable armament, intended for low-level attack against sea and ground targets. Additionally, this mark of Hurricane could carry two 500-lb bombs, or rockets, under the wings.

Denys Gillam, the unrivalled maestro of the low-level attack technique, reckoned that low-level bombing against shipping from a single-seat fighter was too inaccurate. The bombs usually bounced and did not explode. Moreover, rockets were difficult to aim and their electrical mechanisms were faulty.

From Manston he led 615 Squadron until November 25, 1941. During that time it was in continuous action against German coastal convoys.

On September 17 Gillam and his pilots escorted three Blenheims to attack a convoy. The Blenheim was virtually a flying coffin on this type of operation. Two Blenheims were lost from the fire from escorting flak ships. Two Hurricanes were also lost with their pilots. The enemy lost one 4,000-ton ship sunk, two flak ships, and two Me 109s. On September 19, eight Hurricane IIbs (twelve machine guns) and four Hurricane IIcs (four cannons) left one minesweeper on fire and another capsized off Gravelines; on September 26 four Hurricane IIbs and four IIcs sank a 600-ton minesweeper off Dunkirk. This destruction of shipping by these heavily armed Hurricane IIcs continued effectively until the end of November when 615 left Manston.

I discussed low-level attack with Gillam. It was an expensive business. He reckoned that 615 Squadron lost about fifty Hurricanes and fifteen to twenty pilots during its ten weeks at Manston. The German convoys were escorted sometimes by as many as eight flak ships, which were specially built and heavily armed for anti-aircraft duties. Their fire power was considerable and accurate against low-flying attackers who needed to fly straight on the run-in to the target, and could only jink in evasive action as they went away.

Denys gave me this account of his method of attack. 'We approached the target in two sections of four, each section in line abreast, alongside each other; the section leaders were in the middle of this formation of eight. At the right distance from the target, the two leaders throttled back, thus allowing the outside men to get ahead. Then all eight Hurricanes pulled up and dived on the target with cannons and machine-guns blazing. As soon as we passed over it, we were down on the water and jinking away. Out of range, we would re-form and have a second go from a different direction.

'The cast-iron rule was that one Hurricane or even one section of four should never attack alone. By our method, we dispersed the flak and confused the enemy gunners. Not infrequently Me 109s interfered with us. On one such occasion, I was turning behind a 109 and about to get him in my sights, when there was a tremendous bang at my back and I felt my hand hit. I looked around and saw nothing behind me but my number two. On landing back at base, it transpired that this eager beaver had tried to shoot the 109 off my nose and got his deflection wrong. A few days later a call came for volunteers for Murmansk convoy duties. My number two applied, successfully.'

In April 1943, the Air Ministry set up for experienced pilots a special low-flying attack school in Scotland which Denys attended.

This was all in anticipation of the fighter pilots' future role of supporting the Army when it returned to Europe. The combined experience of these battle-hardened professionals provided different, and in some cases more effective, techniques for the future. The favourite weapon was the Hurricane IId, which carried two 40-mm cannon. Gillam said: 'It was deadly accurate, and we vied with each other to achieve the best results.' He added: 'The recoil from these large-calibre cannons was tremendous and reduced the speed by 40 to 50 miles per hour.'

Denys Gillam was a great protagonist of the Hurricane: 'It was the finest gun platform of them all. It also took a staggering amount of punishment and still managed to get home. I have seen pilots bring them back with most of the fin and rudder missing; with a hole in the wing where a Bofors shell had penetrated and taken out the complete ammunition box; indeed any pilot in a Hurricane squadron will recall the extraordinary amount of damage this fighter could absorb and still keep flying.'

This brave and intelligent man left the Hurricane for the newer Hawker ground attack aeroplane, the Typhoon, in July 1943, so he is of no further interest to us in this book! Now in his mid-fifties, he heads his family business, Homfrey Carpets in Halifax, Yorkshire. Quietly spoken, courteous, he dons gold-rimmed glasses on occasion. In his heyday he was known as 'Kill 'em Gillam'.

The weekend flyers

Max Aitken—then and now (Sir Max)

'Weekend flyers' was the name someone before the war gave to the pilots of the Auxiliary squadrons. Soon after the war started there was an amusing story going the rounds of a German pilot being shot down by a 'weekend flyer' in a Gladiator. When picked up and advised of the situation, the unhappy German was reputed to have flung his flying helmet to the ground with the words '*Gott in Himmel*, fancy being shot down by a lawyer in a bloody biplane.'

The Auxiliary Air Force started towards the end of 1925 with the formation of the first four squadrons: 600 (City of London), 601 (County of London), 602 (City of Glasgow), and 603 (City of Edinburgh).

The idea of part-time flyers for the Royal Air Force originated in the mind of Lord Trenchard, founder and father of the R.A.F. and at that time Chief of Air Staff. Because it would not cost much money the politicians raised no objection. It was lucky for our country that these squadrons were established and ready on 3 September 1939.

Spitfires of 603 Squadron destroyed the first German bomber over the British Isles on 16 October 1939, followed by 602 destroying the second enemy fifteen minutes later. A fine start to a great future.

Little has been written about the magnificent part played by these 'amateur' fliers in the early part of the war. In fact, they were as professional as all the rest of us. As the war progressed they ceased to be composed of 'weekend flyers', although they retained their identity as auxiliary squadrons.

Perhaps the most famous of these squadrons

was 601 (County of London). With its home base at Hendon it attracted a number of rich and not-so-rich young men. They were addicted to fast motor cars, winter sports, sailing; some already had the flying bug and owned their own aeroplanes—little ones made by de Havilland, Avro, Percival and Miles. Lord Willoughby de Broke of 605 (County of Warwick) owned a German Klemm. A new light aeroplane in those days could be bought for less than £500. The idea of flying the latest military types with the Royal Air Force had instant appeal to men like these.

I have a special and personal regard for 601 Squadron which goes back to 1932. That summer I was staying with Sir Philip Sassoon at Lympne. He was the Under Secretary of State for Air, and Honorary Air Commodore of 601, which was at summer camp on the aerodrome above his house. With me was Peter Ross, a fellow pilot in 23 Squadron. The C.O. of 601 was Nigel Norman, a well-known pilot and figure in civil aviation at the time. The squadron had an Avro 504 trainer which Norman suggested we might like to fly. I flew it (Peter supposedly the guardian against mishap) to Kenley, the home base of 23 Squadron, to the surprise and delight of my friends there, most of whom had not seen me since that fateful 14 December, six months previously, when I had crashed and lost both legs (I was now staggering about on two tin ones, feeling pretty good).

An amusing aftermath to this episode was told to me many years later by my close friend John Parkes, a founder member of 601, who was a flight commander at the time and was responsible for the Avro. Landing back from a flight and noticing the absence of his much-loved 504, John asked the flight sergeant where it was. The latter replied: 'Dunno, Sir. Some bloke with no legs took it away.' The mystery resolved itself when it returned in the evening, damage free.

Max Aitken, who joined 601 in 1935, has told me a great deal about the squadron. Max, now Sir Max Aitken and Chairman of Beaverbrook Newspapers, had a great wartime career starting as a flight commander in 601. On 6 June, he became the squadron commander, and led his squadron throughout the Battle of Britain with marked success, in spite of the heavy casualties normal at that time.

In 1942 Max Aitken was posted to Headquarters Middle East. This situation did not suit him. His old chief of Fighter Command, Sholto Douglas, was C.-in-C., Middle East. After persistent belly-aching from Max, Sholto gave him 219 Group with responsibility for the eastern Mediterranean from Tripoli in the west to Alexandria and Cairo in the east. It contained a mixed bag of aeroplanes, day and night fighters, strike Beaufighters, the lot. Here was another auxiliary who had come a long way from the weekend flying days.

Max's father, Lord Beaverbrook, was in Churchill's War Cabinet as Minister of Aircraft Production. His personal contribution to the Battle of Britain consisted in galvanizing Whitehall and the industry into increased fighter production. Max inherited some of the characteristics of his redoubtable father which included being outspoken. In Max's case particularly to senior officers—a commendable trait. Like his late father he is a great patriot and a loyal friend.

Another winter sportsman, 'Mouse' Cleaver, got a bullet in his windscreen, from behind. The resultant glass splinters nearly blinded him as he was not wearing goggles. Somehow he managed to get his Hurricane back on to the ground. His sight was permanently affected.

Michael Peacock, a well-known Rugby footballer in 601, died leading his new squadron (a regular one) in France in June 1940 on its first sortie. Peacock was probably the first Auxiliary to lead a regular squadron. Harry Broadhurst, who was the Wing Commander at Lille at the time, told me he saw it all from the ground. Michael and his chaps went straight into an overwhelmingly superior force about to attack the airfield. They had no chance.

In 1940, 601 Squadron reckoned their best pilot was young Willie Rhodes-Moorhouse whose father had won the Victoria Cross in the air during the First World War. Willie died in the Battle of Britain, before—like so many others of his age—he had a chance to prove himself.

Whitney Willard Straight was a highly successful, American-born, racing motorist. He was an undergraduate at Cambridge before the war. A light-aeroplane enthusiast, he joined 601 in 1939. Whitney had an unusual career in the first few months of the war. Talk about quick promotion! On 14 April, Pilot Officer Straight became a Squadron Leader and was hurried off to Norway on a special assignment, in a non-flying capacity. Badly wounded, he was back home on 10 May having relinquished his rank of Squadron Leader. Out of hospital some months later he was gazetted Flying Officer on 3 September 1940. Talk about rapid demotion! However, he was back in the air commanding my old squadron (242) by 21 April 1941. He was a prisoner of war for twelve months from July

1941 until 1942. He finished the war (after somehow returning from being a prisoner of war of the French in 1942) as an Air Commodore commanding 46 Group Transport Command. After the war he became Managing Director of British Overseas Airways Corporation. This intrepid man, in addition to the Distinguished Flying Cross (1941) and the C.B.E. (1944), holds the rare distinction for an airman of having the Military Cross and the Norwegian War Cross for gallantry on the ground.

James McComb joined 607 (County of Durham) in 1933. In August 1940, he was in command of 611 (West Lancashire) Spitfires. I got to know him well, since 611 together with 19 (Spitfires) used to provide top cover for the Duxford Wing. He was a fine leader. He minded about the young inexperienced pilots in his squadron. He survived the war with a good fighting record, having ignored the 'reserved occupation' tag put on him in 1939. Some of his young pilots of those early, strenuous days in that high summer of 1940 lived longer because of James McComb's concern for them.

H.S.L. ('Cocky') Dundas of 616 (South Yorkshire) Spitfires, left the Royal Air Force at the end of the war as a Group Captain covered with decorations. He first flew with me out of Duxford in 1940, then in the Tangmere Wing the following year. He writes in this book, and is now the Managing Director of Rediffusion.

Another Battle of Britain auxiliary was Barry Heath, now Chairman of Triplex. He, too, followed his old C.-in-C., Sholto Douglas, to the Middle East in 1943. In 1940 it became fashionable for industrial firms, and indeed individuals, to make gifts of aeroplanes to the Government. Barry Heath's father gave a Spitfire. This was duly delivered to Hornchurch, where Barry was serving. Hornchurch was not the easiest of airfields, being grass, L-shaped, rutted and small. The day before, Pilot Officer Heath had bent his Spitfire through a miscalculation on landing. Lo and behold the next day a new one arrived—from Dad.

There are many of those splendid weekend fliers whose names I have omitted. They will not mind. Those I have mentioned are representative of the breed so urgently needed thirty-three years ago.

But there is one name that will never be forgotten by his contemporaries in 601 Squadron, nor by any prisoner, like myself, who met him in a P.O.W. camp in Germany. Roger Bushell was shot down in France in early 1940 and captured. He was a barrister and a winter sports enthusiast who favoured the Austrian resorts. He spoke German fluently.

Roger was a dedicated escaper from the moment of his internment. On arrival in Germany, R.A.F. prisoners went to Dulag Luft, near Frankfurt. It was a small camp intended solely as an interrogation place whence people were normally moved fairly quickly into permanent camps. A few British officers, of whom we were all, probably unjustly, highly suspicious, remained for administrative reasons.

Roger made his first escape from there quite soon after arrival, an unheard of impertinence. He had bad luck this first time, getting close to freedom in Switzerland, indeed crossing the frontier back into Germany. This was done later by one or two others at that particular place.

Eventually Roger Bushell arrived at Stalag Luft 3, a large hutted camp near Sagan, in Silesia. This was a camp for all pilots,

Below: pilots of 601 Squadron scramble for their Hurricanes. One of the pilots of this squadron (identity unknown) provided at that time the following vivid combat report:

'I felt a pain in my right thigh, felt the engine stop, heard hissing noises, smelt fumes. My first reaction was to pull back the stick but there was no response. That was at 19,000 feet where the combat ended. The next thing I remember was falling through the air at high speed and feeling my helmet, flying boots, and socks torn off. Lack of oxygen must have dulled my senses. My Hurricane had disappeared. My parachute opened at 7,000 feet. About 2,000 feet lower a Messerschmitt 110 fired at me while being closely pursued by Hurricanes. I landed in the water, just after seeing a motor boat pass about a mile away. My

including those of the U.S.A.F. It was run by the Luftwaffe. From this camp Roger organized and successfully achieved the largest mass escape of the war. No single person was shot during the break out from the camp; seventy made it. In the days that followed most were recaptured, but it caused a great upheaval in the German security arrangements. Every sort of reserve police and home guard was turned out.

The German authorities reacted in typical fashion, in my view with full knowledge of the Luftwaffe. After re-capture, fifty selected escapers were shot, including Roger Bushell, in violation of every civilized code of behaviour. I never knew why Roger was not in Colditz where dedicated escapers were supposed to have been sent. He had caused the Germans more trouble in this respect than anyone ever sent there. Indeed had he gone there he would have been alive today.

The book by Paul Brickhill, *The Great Escape* (and the film which followed), tells faithfully the story of Roger Bushell, a man as British and as tough as the Hurricane fighter he flew with 601 Squadron.

C.O. told me later that they did not see me coming down, although they saw a German parachutist about 200 yards away from me. After about twenty minutes I saw a Hurricane search the bay, and I soon recognised it as belonging to my flight commander. He waved to me and spent some considerable time trying to inform an MTB of my whereabouts, flying backwards and forwards between the boat and me. I was eventually picked up and taken to hospital where my shrapnel wounds were x-rayed and dressed.'

9 MALTA AT BAY

'It makes the Battle of Britain seem like child's play'

At the beginning of 1942 the Luftwaffe returned for the kill. The island was becoming increasingly important on the sea supply route for the North African campaign in which Britain was locked in a life or death struggle with Rommel.

In March the onslaught was at its height. Spitfires flew in from the aircraft carrier *Eagle*. There were fifteen of them. It was planned to employ them in sections of six or four against the enemy fighter escorts, leaving Hurricanes to bring down the bombers. An R.A.F. sergeant manning a fire-tender on one of the airfields described that day:

'The Spitfires came waggling their wings as if to say "O.K., boys, we're here". But that very same evening the gen went round that a big plot was building up over Sicily and within half an hour or so we were to see that Jerry really meant business. Standing at a vantage point in the village of Zurrieq, I saw the first waves of 88s coming all the way over the island. They dived down on Takali where the whole batch of Spits had landed. We

tried to count them as they came in, but it was an utter impossibility. Straight down they went, and one could see the stuff leave the kites before it really got dark.

'The guns were belting rounds up like nothing on earth; tracers filled the sky, and if things weren't so serious one could have called it a lovely sight. The din was terrific and Takali seemed to be ablaze from end to end. The lads would shout that some gun or other had stopped firing, and the crew had been knocked out. But no; they've started again pushing up rounds harder than ever. This time Jerry seemed to be under orders to finish the place and, by hell, he tried his best.'

Despite more raids for the rest of the week, the Spitfires were up in action within three days and had destroyed their first aircraft. But their presence attracted more enemy attacks. By 2 April, no single section of Spitfires was fully operational.

Meanwhile the Germans realized that they could not advance in the desert without getting through supplies from Europe to North Africa. But Malta threatened their convoy routes. For that reason, air power was concentrated in Sicily to try to neutralize the island. If Malta had not held out, these aeroplanes would have been diverted elsewhere.

During April, 6,728 tons of bombs fell on Malta. The dockyards received nearly half, and the three airfields of Luqa, Takali, and Hal Far most of the rest. The people suffered, too, 300 being killed in April alone, with over 10,000 buildings destroyed or damaged. On an average, 170 bombers came over every day, Ju 88s and 87s attacking in waves of twelve to fifteen at a few minute intervals. Three raids a day became typical; the total time spent under alert in April totalled twelve days ten hours and twenty minutes.

One Hurricane squadron had been re-equipped with Spitfires, while a second was converted in April. But many Spitfires were lost on the ground, and it was once more the Hurricane that bore the strain of the battle. Sometimes a dozen Hurricanes would take off to meet a raid of one hundred enemy aircraft. Often the odds grew greater. An R.A.F. corporal wrote:

'During dinner the Hun started again. This time he dropped quite a number of bombs on Luqa village. A direct hit was scored on a shelter. It appeared that water was seeping into the shelter, drowning the people trapped there. The Army and R.A.F. squads were attempting to get through to them. After tea another raid—bombs all over the place. As I am writing, the 6 p.m. news from Blighty can be heard in the sergeants' mess. It makes me just a little homesick. . . .'

Malta at bay! Under the fury of attack, men went out to their work, women tended their homes, the dive-bombers blasted the island, and the R.A.F. struggled on. But by the middle of April, the fighter defence was seriously weakened. The defenders thought themselves lucky if they could put up half a dozen

Previous pages: May 1942: the merchant ship Pampus *burns in Grand Harbour. Below: German aerial photograph of dockyards indicating targets*

aircraft regularly—four to engage the enemy and two for airfield defence. The system used was to scramble the four strikers immediately the warning was received.

'Scramble . . . Scramble . . . Hostile aircraft approaching. . . .'

The fighters would then gain height as rapidly as they could into the sun. To save petrol, the airfield defence pair became airborne at the latest possible moment. Keeping radio silence they flew to a point twenty to thirty miles south of the island. There they gained height until ordered by radio to swoop to which ever airfield was most in need of defence.

During those days of April, the Malta pilots even fought without ammunition! The Germans were never sure when they were really without it—but such was their reputation that the enemy always sheered off just in case.

Ingenuity played its part. April was the month that Pilot Officer 'Humgufery' appeared on the scene. He was the brainchild of Group Captain A. B. Woodhall, the remarkable controller in charge of the Malta Operations Room. On one occasion, all our fighters were grounded to try and increase serviceability. The Huns happened to come over in force with quite a large fighter cover. There were several fighter pilots with Woodhall in the Ops Room at the time, one a Canadian. Woodhall put him at the microphone of a stand-by radio set and proceeded to give him dummy orders. He replied just as if he were flying his fighter! This caused a cry of 'Achtung! Schpitfeuer' to go over the Germans' own radio! And two Me 109s shot each other down without any British aircraft being airborne.

On 15 April the whole island of Malta was awarded the George Cross. On 20 April, Spitfires flew in from the aircraft carrier *Wasp*. They were virtually chased in, forty-seven reaching the island out of an original fifty-four aircraft. The moment they arrived, an attack was launched against them on the ground. While they were still being refuelled, rearmed and serviced, many of them were 'spitchered'. The enemy sent over 300 bombers in one day to destroy them. By the end of the next day, only eighteen were serviceable, and within three days of landing, every single Spitfire had been grounded. Although the enemy lost nearly 200 aircraft in April, the R.A.F. fared worse than usual by comparison—with twenty-three Spitfires lost and fifty-seven damaged, and eighteen Hurricanes lost and thirty damaged. Air raids went on and on. Fighters became fewer. Then the enemy made the fatal blunder of easing up for a few days at the end of the month. Sixty-four Spitfires got through to land on the airfields from 1 a.m. onwards on Saturday 9 May. These had flown off the U.S.S. *Wasp* and H.M.S. *Eagle*.

But the R.A.F. had to be careful not to lose them on the ground before they could go into action. Wing Commander E. J. Cracie later wrote:

'We went to our pilots and ground crew and administrative

staffs and told them we were going to give them, we hoped, an organization which would enable us to win the Battle of Malta, which at that time we were in grave danger of losing. We then told them it would mean the hardest possible work under very difficult conditions, that we were going to enlist the aid of the Army, both in men and materials, but that the battle was lost unless they all pulled their weight one hundred per cent.

'The response was tremendous. Every man felt himself an important item in the battle and not merely an insignificant unit. So magnificently did the ground staffs work that our half-hour service became an absolute outside limit, and the official records show that six Spitfires of one squadron took off to engage the enemy within nine minutes of landing on the island. What a change in 36 hours! Within half an hour, every serviceable Spitfire was in the air. I shall never forget the remark of one airman who, coming out of a slip trench, and seeing two or three squadrons in the air, said "Heavens, look at the fog!" '

In some cases the Spitfires were actually turned round in six minutes. When the enemy came to try to bomb them on the ground, the Luftwaffe were met and attacked by these same aeroplanes in the air. On the ground, each Spitfire was met and directed by a runner to a dispersal pen. Owing to the shortage of petrol bowsers, and all the aircraft having to be refuelled virtually at once, petrol supplies were stored in tins for refuelling by hand. These tins, together with oil, glycol and ammunition, were waiting ready in each pen.

All day long, ground crews, pilots and relief pilots lived in these pens. Army wireless sets, despatch riders and signalmen kept touch among them all. And all day long, too, repair squads were dashing out filling up bomb craters on the runways, while the bombers which had made them were flying back to Sicily.

One of the new Spitfire pilots described his first day:

'Took off from the *Wasp* at 06.45 hours. Landed at Takali at 10.30 hours. The formation leader flew too fast and got his navigation all to hell, so I left them 40 miles west of Bizerta, five miles off the N. African coast, and set course for Malta, avoiding Pantellaria and Bizerta owing to fighters and flak being present there. Jettisoned the long-range tank 20 miles west of Bizerta and reached Malta with twenty gallons to spare in main tank. Of the forty-seven machines that flew off the *Wasp*, one crashed into the sea on take-off, one force landed back on to the deck as he had jettisoned his auxiliary tank in error, one landed in Algeria, one ran out of petrol between Pantellaria and Malta, one crashed on landing at Hal Far, and one crashed off Grand Harbour.

'On landing at Takali I immediately removed my kit, and the machine was rearmed and refuelled. I landed during a raid and four Me 109s tried to shoot me up. Soon after landing, the airfield was bombed but without much damage being done. I was scrambled in a section of four soon after the raid, but we failed to intercept the next one, though we chased several 109s down on the deck. Eat lunch in the aircraft as I was at the ready till dusk. After lunch we were heavily bombed again by eight Ju 88s.

'Scrambled again in the same section after tea—no luck again. One Spit was shot down coming in to land and another one at the edge of the airfield. Score for the day, seven confirmed, seven probables and fourteen damaged for the loss of three Spits.

'The tempo of life here is just indescribable. The morale of all is magnificent—pilots, ground crew and Army, but life is certainly tough. The bombing is continuous on and off all day. One lives here only to destroy the Hun and hold him at bay; everything else, living conditions, sleep, food, and all the ordinary standards of life have gone by the board. It all makes the Battle of Britain and fighter sweeps seem like child's play in comparison, but it is certainly history in the making, and nowhere is there aerial warfare to compare with this.'

There were nine air-raids that day. The 'fog' of Spitfires began to show results within hours. Eight enemy planes were destroyed —plus many probables. A shock of excitement and exultation shivered through everyone.

The next day was destined to be another milestone for Malta: the climax of the battle if not its end. The minelaying cruiser H.M.S. *Welshman*, capable of 40 knots, was due to berth in Grand Harbour soon after dawn. The enemy would be sure to try to sink her. At 5.45 a.m. an alert sounded, but it was no more than an enemy reconnaissance. The Luftwaffe came in force that day. But the Germans were due for no fewer than three shocks—a smokescreen, a blistering barrage, and squadrons of Spitfires. All these precautions were necessary as the cruiser carried a cargo mainly of ammunition, which was unloaded in five hours.

H.M.S. Eagle—*Spitfires flew off this carrier to reinforce the defence of Malta*

Smoke containers were brought ashore first, and these augmented the smoke generators in use for the first time in Grand Harbour. The smokescreen was started at a signal from the Fighter Ops Room. The harbour area had overall priority for the gun barrage, specially sited to cover the cruiser. The R.A.F. fighters were warned that the barrage would continue regardless of their whereabouts!

10. 56 a.m.—the heaviest raid of the day. Twenty Stukas and ten Ju 88s came escorted by Me 109s. The enemy dived as low as they dared, dropping some forty tons of bombs over the Grand Harbour zone. One was a near miss for the *Welshman*, still being unloaded.

Thirty-seven Spitfires and thirteen Hurricanes went up to intercept. Fifty fighters, an unheard of number. As the first wave of Ju 88s dived out of the sun, the fighters were already 'mixing it' with them. Combats developed all over the sky. Then the Ju 87s sailed in from the east. The harbour barrage erupted— and the Spitfires jumped on them, many Spits following Stukas through their own barrage.

In the afternoon came another attack, but by then the ship had unloaded its cargo. The same drill met the raiders: smoke, fire and fighters. The evening brought a two-wave raid, first a high-level attack by Cant 1007s and then Stukas.

The same pilot who described his first day on Malta had this to say about the second:

'We climbed to 4,000 feet, and then the barrage was put up by the harbour defences and the cruiser. The C.O. dived down into it and I followed close on him. We flew three times to and fro in the barrage, trusting to luck to avoid the flak. Then I spotted a Ju 87 climbing out of the fringe of the barrage and I turned and chased him. I gave him a one-second burst of cannon and he broke off sharply to the left. At that moment another Ju 87 came up in front of my nose and I turned into him and I let him have it.

'Screwball' Beurling—one of the most unusual aces of all, and top-notch pilot of the Malta campaign. Below: naval pilot runs to his Hurricane, 1942

His engine started to pour out black smoke and he started weaving. I kept the button pushed hard, and after a further two- or three-second burst with the one cannon I had left, the other having jammed, he keeled over at 1,500 feet and went into the drink.

'I then spotted a 109 firing at me from behind and pulled the kite round to port, and after one and a half turns got on his tail. Before I could fire, another 109 cut across my bows from the port side and I turned straight on his tail and fired, till my cannon stopped through lack of "ammo". He was hit and his engine poured out black smoke, but I had to beat it as I was now defenceless and two more 109s were attacking me.

'I spiralled straight down to the sea at full throttle, and then weaved violently toward the land with the two 109s still firing at me. I went under the fringe of the smokescreen to try to throw them off, but when I came out the other side I found them both sitting up top waiting for me. I therefore kept right down at nought feet and steep-turned towards them, noticing the smoke from their gun ports as I did so. After about five minutes of this, I managed to throw them off. I landed back at Takali and made out my report, claiming an 87 destroyed and one Me 109 damaged.'

There were 110 Spitfire sorties and fourteen Hurricane sorties on that day, 10 May 1942. They destroyed fifteen attackers, and ack-ack shot down a further eight. Three Spitfires were lost but two of the pilots saved, so that *Welshman* had been protected from enemy air attack for the loss of one pilot. After that the Germans made fewer daylight raids but more by night. Their losses were still substantial.

June saw the arrival on the Malta scene of one of the most unusual aces of all, George 'Screwball' Beurling. A real lone-wolf fighter pilot from Canada, Beurling disliked discipline and routine. Not surprisingly, therefore, he had had a chequered if colourful career by the time he joined 249 Squadron on the island.

He started scoring seriously on 6 July and in a matter of a few weeks Screwball became the top-notch pilot of the entire Malta campaign. One of his eccentricities was that he had been offered a commission on several occasions but had refused to take it. Eventually, at some stage that year he was simply informed that he had been commissioned!

After bringing down many of the enemy, Screwball Beurling destroyed a Junkers 88 on 14 October 1942, before himself being hit. Despite this, he shot down two more Me 109s before baling out with a wounded heel. He fell into the sea, was rescued, and recovered in hospital. A little later, he was being flown home in a Liberator when it crashed into the sea while trying to land at Gibraltar. The aircraft broke in half, but Beurling was one of the few to survive, breaking a leg. Later in the war, he flew again in the European theatre. He died on 20 May 1948 while piloting a Mitchell aircraft to Israel.

The battle for Malta still raged but now more in our favour. A new plan was introduced, of intercepting enemy bombers before they could reach Malta, and this in time tilted the scales still further. But the inevitable result of this plan was that pilots and aeroplanes were liable to come down in the Mediterranean, and so the Air-Sea Rescue Service became more vital than ever. This is a typical story from a high-speed launch log:

'At 11 a.m. we had a call out in HSL 128 for a Spitfire pilot, said to have baled out on a bearing of 160 Hal Far, about 100 yards out. Sounded like a piece of cake, for even though enemy fighters were plentiful in the vicinity, the position given was close to the island and we now had Spitfires on the job as well as Hurricanes. Getting on the given bearing, we steamed 100, 200, 300 yards—still nothing seen—and kept on going, though enemy activity was getting more and more lively overhead.

'After we had steamed out about three miles, one of the escorting Hurricanes was shot down a couple of miles ahead of us. It was while we were investigating this wreckage that Jerry got closest to us, but even then the bullets only churned up the water one hundred feet away. As there was no survivor from this crash and still no sign of the original pilot for whom we had been called out, I decided to make for base, but on our way back we saw another fighter crash about six miles over to the westward and a parachute drifting down. We picked this pilot up within a few minutes of his hitting the water, and he turned out to be a Hun—a cheery soul who advised us to get back ashore before we were hurt.

'As we were then fairly well out, I decided to run out and then come in on our original bearing from a distance of about ten miles, as even the worst possible estimate of distance could hardly be over ten miles out. We actually found the Spitfire pilot in his dinghy about nine miles from the land, and the German pilot insisted upon shaking hands with him as he welcomed him aboard.'

Malta was still besieged, short of food, battered, and bombed. The convoys still had to claw their way to and from the island. As late as 11 October 1942, fifty-eight bombers blasted Malta, and during the next week there were nearly 250 raiders by day. But on 23 October came Rommel's defeat, while soon after the Americans invaded from the west. The Allies were soon sweeping across North Africa from both ends. At long last, the siege was raised.

It was from Malta that Spitfire fighter-bombers first flew. They carried 250-pounders for bombing raids on enemy airfields in Sicily. They were symbolic of the switch from the defensive to the offensive in the Mediterranean as elsewhere.

Malta postscript by 'Laddie' Lucas

A factual account of this tremendous campaign is written by Wing Commander P. B. 'Laddie' Lucas, D.S.O., D.F.C. I quote it in his words.

Lucas—1942

'During March and April [1942] all the heat was turned on Malta, and remorseless air attacks by day and night wore the island down and pressed it to the last gasp.' (Sir Winston Churchill, *The Hinge of Fate*.)

The crunch of the air battle for Malta came in the spring and early summer of 1942. What was at stake then was survival—survival for the Hurricane and Spitfire squadrons and their tough, seasoned ground crews, for the Maltese people themselves, and for the island as a festering thorn in Rommel's side as its shore-based, strike aircraft harassed his seaborne reinforcements battling their way across the Mediterranean to the Western Desert and the formidable Afrika Korps.

I doubt whether there was a fighter pilot on the stricken airfields of Takali, Luqa and Hal Far who did not recognize at this sombre moment in the conflict the extent of the danger to the island's life—or, indeed, the need, no matter what the cost, somehow to hang on.

For weeks a handful of Hurricane IIs, aided by Group Captain A. B. Woodhall's masterly controlling, had been meeting, against all the odds, the rising crescendo of Field Marshal Kesselring's relentless attacks on Grand Harbour and the airfields.

Outnumbered, usually, by twelve or fourteen to one and, later—with the arrival of the Me 109fs in Sicily—outperformed, the pilots of the few old aircraft which the ground crews struggled valiantly to keep serviceable, went on pressing their attacks, ploughing their way through the German fighter screens—and our flak—to close in with the Ju 87s and 88s as they dived for their targets.

For the new arrival from England, fresh from flying Spitfire Vs in Fighter Command, it was a rugged baptism. But it couldn't go on. Kesselring now had at his disposal in Sicily some 600 front-line aircraft against, perhaps, twenty or thirty serviceable fighters of our own. Some means would have to be found to reinforce the squadrons with new Spitfire Vs if the island, and its tiny air force, were to be saved.

To send replacements by sea was out of the question. The March convoy, which had tried to run the gauntlet from Alexandria, had ended in disaster. To the west, Kesselring's command of the Narrows made the risks of a seaborne reinforcement from Gibraltar quite unacceptable. In these bleak days, with Malta's food down to six weeks' supplies, our daily ration in 249 Squadron began to dwindle ominously. Diminishing quantities of bully beef, monotonously supported by bitter bread, with "butter" made from goat's milk—garry grease the pilots called it—did not make a good base for combat. The gathering weight of crisis was felt by all.

It was against this fast-deteriorating background that the great carrier-borne reinforcing operation was undertaken from the west. Winston Churchill's personal intervention with the President had secured for the Allies the use of the massive American carrier, *Wasp*, with its critical ability to house forty-eight Spitfires against *Eagle*'s sixteen. The Royal Navy, Royal Air Force and United States Navy worked together as one.

I recall, with undiminished vividness, a singular adventure which occurred when our turn came to fly the Spitfire Vbs, with their two cannons and four machine guns, off *Eagle* while our forty-eight comrades, a mile or two to the south, were flying off *Wasp*.

The take-off point was just north of Algiers, the distance from Malta 667 miles. Flying time was 3 hours and 30 minutes at a height of 10,000 feet. Our instructions from the admirable W/Cdr. J. S. McLean, an officer of unusual efficiency and spirit, who conducted these operations with signal success for the Royal Air Force, were clear cut and direct.

'After take-off climb to 2,000 feet; switch on to the 90-gallon overload tank and switch off the main tanks.

'If, by chance, your overload tank doesn't work you have two choices. Either gain height and bale out, in which case the Navy ought to be able to pick you up. Or, if you don't fancy that, then fly south into North Africa, destroy the aircraft and get off back home. In no circumstances try to land back on the carrier.'

Spitfire Vb on Malta, 1942

I was just setting course with my flight of aircraft from *Eagle* when down below I spotted a Spitfire circling *Wasp*, now steaming flat-out in a twinkling, sunlit sea, with a wind speed of perhaps 45 or 50 knots over the deck. One pass over the ship and now the pilot was turning in tight towards the flight deck on his final approach. I couldn't believe it; I wondered who it could be with that sort of nerve. No hooks, no arresting gear . . .

The Spitfire seemed almost to be hanging in the air having little more speed than the ship. But now it was on the flight deck . . . rolling . . . rolling . . . rolling. Then, blessed relief, it was still. There were only a few feet to spare.

Several hours later, Pilot Officer Smith, a quiet Canadian of engaging charm, joined us in Malta, jubilant at becoming the first man to land a Spitfire, unaided, on the deck of a carrier.

But he had yet another 'first' to claim. On landing, they had taken him straight down to the wardroom where, of course, in accordance with the best traditions of the U.S. Navy, no alcohol was to be found. Within moments a large glass of whisky was being pressed furtively into his hand!

Wasp's second run with the Spitfires had proved even more telling than the first. Churchill sent a personal message to her Captain and crew:

'Who said a wasp couldn't sting twice.'

The tide of battle was beginning to turn, and as the pendulum started to swing back, a Canadian sergeant pilot, of rare ability and personality, joined us in 249.

George Beurling, by any test, was exceptional. He was exceptionally untidy.

exceptionally imprecise in his discipline and exceptionally individualistic. He possessed a penchant for calling everything and everyone —the Maltese, the 109s, the flies—those 'goddam screwballs'. The name stuck. Somehow nothing else but 'Screwball' would have fitted the man.

A combination of attributes placed Beurling in front of the rest. He was an outstanding shot, getting the very most out of his Spitfire as a superbly steady gun platform. It was an art which he had perfected with practice and infinite patience after intense technical study. I used to wonder sometimes how good he would have been at driven partridges in November.

Beyond that, his reflexes were like quicksilver and he had a pair of strikingly blue eyes, beneath a shock of fair, tousled hair, which penetrated the Mediterranean glare and the haze of the upper air, as no other pilot's did. Screwball had the best eyesight of any man I have ever known.

I can hear that scratchy, transatlantic voice now, rasping over the RT, as we manoeuvred up-sun:

'Tiger Leader, 109s at 2 o'clock same level; 88s a couple of thousand feet below. . . . There are a helluva lot of the goddam screwballs. . . .'

And then the rest of us would spot them. The seconds his wonderful eyes gained him gave him a priceless advantage in combat. His commanding control over his Spitfire and his precision shooting did the rest. But, strangely, it was his meticulous honesty in reporting his numerous claims which left the most indelible impression.

I remember one day in July the squadron had had a brush with some 109s sweeping in high over the island after a bombing raid. Beurling had sent one down flaming into the sea off St Paul's Bay. Then, way down below, his eye fastened on an Italian Macchi 202 heading north for Sicily on its own. Screwball attacked with machine guns alone, having used up all his cannon ammunition. Then he broke away and landed.

To the waiting Intelligence Officer he reported the destruction of a 109, having seen it crash into the sea. After that he had attacked a Macchi, seeing strikes behind the cockpit, in the engine and along the port wing. But he could only claim 'one damaged' as he had had to break away and had not seen what had happened to the aircraft.

Some while later, a Macchi 202 was reported to have force-landed on Gozo, a small island, just north of Malta. It had been hit behind the cockpit and in the port wing, but not in the engine. When they gave Screwball the news

Lucas today—Chairman G.R.A. Property Trust Ltd

and told him his claim had been updated to 'one destroyed', his face showed no emotion whatever. 'Dammit,' he muttered, dead pan, 'I was certain I hit that goddam screwball in the engine!'

The arrival of the Spitfires and the successes they achieved had given an immense lift to Malta's morale; but even in the darkest days the courage and the faith of the Maltese women never wavered.

I recall, soon after the second lot of reinforcements had landed from *Eagle*, being hit ignominiously in the glycol tank by a cannon shell from a 109 in circumstances which are best left unsaid.

Aided by fortune rather than skill, I contrived to coax the Spitfire back across the coast, and, with a dead stick and a fair quantity of smoke emerging from the coolant tank, landed the aircraft wheels up, in a small cornfield in the south-west of the island.

Three old Maltese women, in long dresses with black scarves over their heads, were working in the field. As I climbed out of the cockpit into the dusty heat of the day one of them came stumbling over the rough ground towards me. She stared anxiously into my face. Tears, not words, spelled out her relief.

With simple dignity she laid her hand first on the wing of the aircraft and then on my arm. As she did so she made the sign of the cross, devoutly and deliberately, across her chest. A smile of benign tranquillity spread over that kindly, ageing face. For a moment, in a blessed Malta field, the Roman and the Anglican Churches were as one.

133

The introduction of the Sea Hurricane was foreshadowed by the short-lived defence of Norway in early 1940. In April, the Germans invaded this neutral country. The British Government at once sent units of the Royal Navy, the Army, and the Royal Air Force to try to help.

Towards the end of April, two fighter squadrons, 263 (Gladiators—Squadron Leader Jack Donaldson), and 46 (Hurricanes—Squadron Leader K. B. B. Cross), went out aboard the aircraft carrier H.M.S. *Glorious*. The Hurricanes were unable to use the available landing strip which was too small for them, and went back home. The Gladiators were therefore on their own and fighting successfully until May 26, when the Hurricanes returned and landed at Bardufoss, near Narvik.

The Hurricane squadron was instantly successful in its destruction of enemy aircraft. The Norwegian campaign was, however, short. On 3 June, evacuation of the British from Narvik began, ending four days later. The two fighter squadrons fought continuously and valiantly during this time. Then the remaining pilots and aircraft embarked on the *Glorious* for home. Hurricanes had never previously landed on a carrier. 46 Squadron had ten out of the original eighteen left. 'Bing' Cross decided to 'land them on'.

All arrived safely. An amazing achievement.

The *Glorious*, however, was intercepted and sunk by the German warships *Scharnhorst* and *Gneisenau*, with the total loss of 263 Squadron and 46 Squadron except for Squadron Leader Cross and Flight Lieutenant Jamieson (from New Zealand). After many hours on a Carley float, they were rescued by a ship and put ashore on the Faroes. Both these exceptional characters continued to increase their reputations throughout the war, Jamie Jamieson retiring as a Wing Commander, while 'Bing' Cross served with distinction in the Western Desert and Europe, retiring some years ago as Air Chief Marshal Sir Kenneth Cross.

I remember in July 1940, when I was at Duxford with 242 Squadron, Squadron Leader Cross arriving there after his Arctic exploit, and hobbling across to greet me. I said, 'What's the matter with you?' to receive the succinct reply, 'Bit of frostbite, old boy.'

It is fitting to record that Jack Donaldson, who died in the *Glorious*, was eldest of three brothers, the others being Teddy and Arthur, who were each awarded the D.S.O. for gallantry in the air during the war. A remarkable family record. The latter two survived the war.

This initial experience was a pointer to the future. The Hurricane, without modification, and without special training for the pilots, had successfully landed ten times on the deck of a

IO SEA HURRICANE
The achievement of the 'Hurricats'

Previous pages: Sea Hurricane Mark Ia. An explosion of 150 lbs of cordite fired the 'Hurricat' off the ship. The pilot's job was to deal with air attack on convoys. After that, he had to ditch the aeroplane in the sea or—if he was lucky—make for land

carrier; each time with a different pilot and at his first attempt. 46 was a good fighter squadron with an outstanding leader, but this was really remarkable.

The Battle of Britain occupied everyone's attention for the next three months. When it was over, the makers of the Hurricane—Hawker's—were asked to examine the possibility of modifying this fighter so that it could be fired, catapulted, or rocket-propelled off a ship. The object of the exercise was to provide some protection for convoys against air attack. The Admiralty arranged for the necessary equipment for the ship; and early in 1941 a 'hooked Hurricane' duly arrived from Hawker's at the Royal Aircraft Establishment, Farnborough, for evaluation in its new role. It worked. Fifty Hurricanes were converted for catapulting; and thirty-five merchant ships were fitted with the necessary launching gear.

The idea was that each of these ships would carry a Hurricane and form one of the convoy. When air attack became imminent, the Hurricane would be launched to deal with the enemy. The genius sitting on his backside in Whitehall who conceived this scheme had forgotten that the Hurricane carried a pilot. What about him when he had finished with the enemy? Fly to the nearest land? Not much good for a short-range single-engined fighter in the Arctic or the Atlantic. Well, bale out and let the convoy pick him up. That is exactly what these splendid chaps did. A personal account of this operation has been written for me by Air Vice Marshal Michael Lyne. We served together in 19 Squadron (Spitfires) at Duxford in February and March 1940. Michael was one of the early volunteers for this dangerous but fascinating type of operation.

'At the beginning of 1941 a secret letter was sent around Fighter Command requesting pilots for a contemplated new sea-going force known as the Merchant Fighter Unit. The idea of such a duty appealed to me so I applied to join it.

'When my squadron commander got my application he said, "Michael, you're mad". However, I was accepted and two months later found myself sitting in the cockpit of a Hurricane high in the bows of a merchant ship in the Clyde. The ship was rumbling along at about twelve knots and a bunch of cheerful-looking characters were leering at me through armour-plated windows— the final stages of preparing to be catapulted off the ship in my Hurricane by the explosion of some 150 lbs of cordite. Perhaps my squadron commander had been right. Anyhow, it was too late to worry about it now. In the event, it was not so violent as I had imagined.

'The birth of this Merchant Fighter Unit had been the result of German long-range four-engined Condor bombers attacking British convoys with a certain amount of success. These enemy aircraft operated outside the range of our land-based fighters and the only resistance they had was light, inaccurate anti-aircraft fire. There were enough merchant ships being lost through submarines without enemy aircraft joining in to increase such casualties. The only way to cope with them was by fighters—the problem was how to operate them. In quick time a rocket-type catapult was designed which was simple and light enough to be used on merchant ships.

'It could be operated by quickly trained crews. Within a month such a device had been designed, built, and tested. By early summer 1941 the first merchant ships were carrying the Hurricane together with an R.A.F. crew trained to work the catapult. Our orders were simple: "To defend the convoy itself against German bombers." Having destroyed or frightened the enemy away from the convoy it was recommended to the pilot that if he could not make land he should bale out and the Royal Navy would pick him up. It was all good stuff and no doubt sounded splendid to the chap sitting on his bottom in Whitehall. To be fair, it worked sometimes.

'The German U-boats tended to pick out the Hurricane-armed merchant ships for their first torpedo salvoes. This was occasionally a problem for R.A.F. personnel on board who were unaccustomed to ships. As a result, one or two were sometimes lost falling down hatches from which the covers had been blown by the force of the torpedo explosion. Additionally, when the ship was abandoned, pilots, officers of the Royal Navy who manned the Operations Rooms, together with their merchant seamen comrades all finished up in the same life-boats. Life indeed could be interesting.

'Nevertheless successes there were. Few fighter units can have recorded a higher proportion of kills to the number of take-offs.

'Sadly the first success was a bitter one. Flying Officer Kendal took to the air from a Russian-bound convoy in the Arctic. He shot down an enemy aircraft, but in the ensuing bale-out his parachute failed to open and he died.'

Successes continued at intervals, some in the hopelessly out-numbered conditions met by these northern convoys off the Norwegian coast. One Hurricane against forty enemy torpedo- and dive-bombers was not abnormal. In other areas the Hurricane pilot would be up against one, or at the most two, soft-skinned long-range German bombers which he could easily shoot down.

The records show there were a number of successful combats, but these were only secondary in importance in the long-term objective which was to stop enemy air attack on convoys. This was achieved. After the introduction of the 'Hurricats', air attacks on convoys showed a marked decline.

Despite many difficulties, the scheme prospered modestly, and May 1942 saw the introduction of the Sea Hurricane Mk llc (four cannons). A couple of months later the Navy had nearly

Michael Lyne—then and now

137

600 Sea Hurricanes: 200 were serving afloat, while eighty flew on duties from various bases ashore.

It was also intended to use Spitfires in this role, but before it could happen the unit was disbanded, as a result of the greater availability of aircraft carriers.

Sea Hurricanes were used on some bigger aircraft carriers, one of their best-known actions being in the famous Malta convoy of August 1942. The convoy left Gibraltar on 10 August, comprising fourteen merchant ships, with a formidable escort of two battleships, seven cruisers, twenty-four destroyers, and aircraft carriers *Eagle*, *Indomitable*, and *Victorious*. There were seventy naval fighter aircraft including thirty-nine Sea Hurricanes. The enemy attacked almost at once—with U-boats below the surface and 500 aircraft above it. Sea Hurricanes, Fulmars, and Martlets all tried to stem the onslaught. When the *Eagle* went down, she took ten aircraft with her. The fight went on for four days before the convoy finally reached the umbrella of Beaufighters flying a long way out from Malta. By then, sea-air fighters had claimed thirty-nine enemy aircraft for eight of ours.

A single Sea Hurricane pilot, Lieutenant Cork D.F.C., destroyed three German aircraft and three Italian, during these four momentous days.

Dickie Cork was one of the naval pilots seconded to squadrons in Fighter Command at the beginning of the Battle of Britain. He joined my squadron (242) and flew alongside me throughout that period. Towards the end of the battle he was awarded the Distinguished Flying Cross, the first naval pilot to be so decorated. We received the usual telegram from the Air Ministry to the effect that His Majesty the King, on the recommendation of the Commander-in-Chief, had been graciously pleased to award the Distinguished Flying Cross to Sub-Lieutenant R. Cork, R.N. We celebrated, and pinned the ribbon on his chest. A couple of days later a second telegram was received, this time from the Admiralty. It said: 'For Distinguished Flying Cross read Distinguished Service Cross.' The latter is the Royal Navy's equivalent to the Army's Military Cross (M.C.) and the Royal Air Force's D.F.C. Through the proper channels we firmly expressed non-comprehension. The King had given him the D.F.C.; only His Majesty could change it. Corky continued to wear his D.F.C. While this exchange continued, we received a visit from the Air Minister, Sir Archibald Sinclair, to whom we told our tale. He assured us of his support, declaring that we were absolutely right.

After the Battle of Britain, Dickie Cork and Jimmy Gardner (our splendid 'Wavy Navy' pilot) were posted back to a Fleet Air Arm unit at Barrow-in-Furness. During his time with us Corky had acquired four buttons from the tunics of fellow pilots in the Duxford Wing. These he wore as the left row of his double-breasted naval tunic. From top to bottom they were an R.A.F.

button, a Royal Canadian Air Force button, a Czech Air Force button, and a Polish Air Force button. The last named was in silver and particularly conspicuous, as all the rest on his tunic were golden.

A week or so after his departure, Corky flew in to see us. As he walked towards us we noticed with horror that he was properly dressed, and worse still he was wearing the ribbon of the D.S.C. instead of our D.F.C.

He told us that soon after his arrival at Barrow, he encountered an Admiral whom he saluted, intending to pass on. The Admiral stopped him, pointed at the purple and white diagonal stripes of his D.F.C. ribbon and asked, 'What's that?' Respectfully, Sub-Lieutenant Cork told him. The Admiral's gaze shifted to his tunic with its row of exotic buttons. His face suffused, then became empurpled. There was, Corky assured us, 'an unparalleled scene'. Since then he had been correctly dressed as an officer in the Royal Navy.

The last time I saw him was in the summer of 1941 at Tangmere. He had flown in with a bearded friend called 'Butch'. The Tangmere Wing was due over northern France two hours later. We put them each in a Spitfire and took them with us. Like old times Corky flew alongside me.

Dickie Cork died later in an accident at night over Trincomalee (Ceylon). In his confidential report when he left 242 Squadron I had written: 'He is one of the finest young officers I have ever known.'

But to return to the Sea Hurricane; its heyday was passing. The final occasion recorded in which Sea Hurricanes saw action was towards the end of the Russian convoy coded PQ18. Air attacks opened on PQ18 the moment that the ships came within the range of the northerly German air bases in Norway. But the enemy did not find things easy. They were met by a dozen Sea Hurricanes flown off the escort carrier *Avenger*. The respective losses were five Luftwaffe to four Sea Hurricanes. But all except one of our pilots were saved. The convoy got through more or less unscathed.

Sea Hurricanes were used on the larger aircraft carriers. Here a Mark Ib leaves H.M.S. Argus

II M DIT RAN AN O
From the desert to the Alps

In the summer of 1940, there was one Hurricane in the entire Middle East, its guns no longer serviceable because of desert sand. Someone had the bright idea of flying it from place to place in an effort to convince our Italian adversaries that we had modern aeroplanes reaching Egypt!

But more convincing evidence would be needed eventually. It was as well that our air power in the Middle East was augmented by the setting up of Takoradi, on what used to be called the Gold Coast in West Africa, as a port of 'débarquement' for Hurricanes—which were then put together and flown to Egypt and the front line.

Hurricanes came to the fore in the Western Desert as early as 18 November 1941, when Operation Crusader began, with the intention of relieving Tobruk, then under siege. The Luftwaffe harried the relieving forces, but Hurricane bombers of 33 and 80 Squadrons got eight without loss. The battle swayed dramatically. First Rommel found a couple of his precious Panzer divisions in danger, but then a little afterwards the Allies were once more cut off from Tobruk. Relentless attacks from the air, however, caused the Germans to withdraw.

On 29 November 1941 in the midst of this air activity, Flying Officer P. T. Cotton was piloting an unarmed Hurricane on recce over El Adem. This airfield was occupied by the Germans. Two Me 109s attacked him for half an hour, but despite his vulnerability, he managed to evade them by skilful flying. They used all their ammunition and were forced to leave. Unluckily the Hurricane's engine gave up when Cotton was only about fifteen miles from his base—but this did not deter him from putting the fighter down in a good landing on the sand, without any damage to himself or it.

During December 1941, Rommel was trying to form a line of defence with Gazala as his basis. The Luftwaffe was covering his Afrika Korps as they retreated towards this line. In the course of the ground operations, a fierce air battle erupted, with a squadron of Hurricanes taking on a score of Me 109s plus some Fiats for good measure. A South African pilot had to bale out after getting a shot in his glycol tank. Flight Lieutenant Tracey watched him parachute to the desert between the opposing ground armies and decided to do something about it. He landed his own Hurricane, picked up his colleague, and bore him back on his lap! Then a week after this, another Hurricane saw a similar situation, when a Ju 87 landed to try and save a fellow-pilot forced down in the desert in his Junkers. But the Hurricane destroyed the two Junkers.

In May 1942 the first fighter squadron of the R.A.F. Desert Air Force received its Spitfire Vbs. The maximum operational height of the Vb was 36,000 feet. At this stage the movement of Allied shipping in Alexandria and the Suez Canal was of much importance to the Germans. As a result the Germans were sending over Egypt high-flying, photographic reconnaissance aircraft to keep them informed of Allied movements. These flew at 37,000 feet or higher, safe from interception, and always at the same time of the day. One of the essential elements of desert air warfare was the repair and modification of aircraft for operational or special duties. This was the job of R.A.F. Maintenance Units, of which the best known was No 103 Aboukir. This M.U. got fed up with these high-flying Germans and decided to do something about them. They selected a new Spit Vc (a Vb with a different undercarriage), lightened it by removing cannons and machine guns, leaving only two machine guns; increased the engine compression to give it more power in rarefied air; fitted a four-bladed propeller; and extended the wing tips thereby increasing the lift.

A German high-flyer was duly intercepted by one of 103 M.U.'s pilots at 37,000 feet, pursued and shot down at 42,000 feet.

Not long after this a second was shot down at 45,000 feet, followed by a third and last at 50,000 feet. After this the enemy ceased their high-altitude reconnaissance.

These converted Spitfires were not pressurized which makes the endurance of the pilots quite amazing. Any fighter pilot will recall the discomfort of unpressurized flying over 30,000 feet. During this period of activity at 103 M.U., a pressurized Spitfire VI was delivered from England but it could not compete with the locally modified Vs. Anyhow success had been achieved.

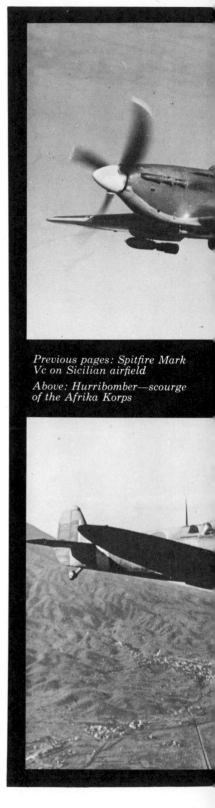

Previous pages: Spitfire Mark Vc on Sicilian airfield

Above: Hurribomber—scourge of the Afrika Korps

Meanwhile during the autumn of 1942 the respective ground and air forces were girding their loins for the El Alamein offensive. Montgomery led the Eighth Army on the ground; Tedder commanded the Western Desert Air Force. Hurricanes formed much of Tedder's close-support force, though conversion had started to Kittyhawks as well as Spitfires.

The historic El Alamein artillery barrage began on the night of 23–24 October 1942. Troops advanced, Wellingtons went for enemy armour, while 73 Squadron Hurricanes took to the desert night air, shooting up everything they could find.

The battle blazed for five days. The three types of fighter forced Ju 87s to jettison their loads, sometimes over their own troop areas. Ground attack Hurricanes scourged the desert and the enemy. Eleven squadrons took part in the whole affair from 23 October to 8 November. Just six squadrons of Hurricanes claimed the following: thirty-nine tanks, 212 lorries and armoured troop carriers, twenty-six bowsers, forty-two guns, 200 other vehicles, and four small ammunition fuel dumps! They flew 842 sorties in the seventeen days for the loss of eleven pilots.

The breaking point came on 4 November, when both the Germans and Italians started a retreat that became a rout. Fighter-bombers found the westbound roads so cluttered with these columns that they could scarcely miss their targets.

Below: Spitfire Mark IXs over Italy. From the end of 1942 this superb fighter began superseding the Mark V in squadron service

Even after flying back to base for more supplies to feed their weapons and fuel tanks, the fighters came across the identical targets in practically the same spots as they had left them.

Meanwhile Spitfires proved predominant in the Anglo-American landings of Operation Torch on 8 November. This was the amphibious operation aimed around Algiers—far west of the German lines in North Africa. Spitfires Mk Vb had been assembled at Gibraltar ready for this Algiers landing, both Spitfires and Hurricanes being put together for this role.

The first fighters actually employed in Torch were 43 Squadron Hurricanes, in a light bombing capacity, but Spitfire squadrons were not far behind over Maison Blanche, Algiers. Another Hurricane squadron and four Spitfire squadrons participated, and the Americans also flew Spitfires. The Royal Navy Seafires —Sea Spitfires—saw action too. Two dozen had been aboard H.M.S. *Furious* and Lt. G. C. Baldwin R.N. took the credit for the first Seafire success of all.

Meanwhile the Eighth Army was closing the gap between the two Allied spheres of influence. They took the vital Castel Benito airfield, Tripoli, on 23 January 1943. This particular phase is memorable for the fact that twenty-three Hurricanes flew far ahead of our advancing army and landed at airfields actually behind the retreating enemy. From these airfields they assaulted the disordered enemy, either destroying or at least damaging 300 vehicles.

By March 1943, Hurricanes were entrenched at Castel Benito, using it as a base point for their onslaught against the Germans' Mareth line defences. On 10 March, just a dozen anti-tank Hurricanes knocked out six tanks, thirteen armoured vehicles, ten lorries, five half-tracks, gun and trailer, and a wireless van. They sustained not a single loss to themselves. About the end of the month came the long-awaited link-up between the Eighth Army and the American II Corps. On 22 April, Spitfires shot down twenty-one fully loaded Me 323s, which were making a final, frantic attempt to fly through to the Germans with supplies to keep them going. And Spitfires together with Warhawks caught great air convoys of Junkers 52/3Ms and Me 323s crammed with fuel for the enemy. By May it was all over.

The story of the Spitfire and Hurricane in the Mediterranean theatre naturally followed the pattern of the war there. After North Africa the invasion of Sicily came—and a new Spitfire. From the latter months of 1942, Spitfires Mk IX began superseding Mk Vs in squadron service. Unlike the Mk Vs, they had a more symmetrical shape. Hornchurch and Biggin Hill squadrons were among the early recipients, but the Mk IX was also being sent overseas. Drop tanks were also fitted to Spitfires around this stage, giving them longer range. Later still, Rolls Royce evolved the Mk XII by adapting the Mk VIII fuselage to take a Griffon engine.

Supporting invasion of southern France: Spitfire returning from a sortie. Typhoon in background.

So Spitfires Mk V and Mk IX of 92 Squadron arrived at Sicily on 15 July 1943, within a week of the Allied landings there. On the fourth anniversary of the war, 3 September, came the crossing of the Straits of Messina in Italy and within a further week the Salerno landings by the British and Americans. Spitfires provided short-period fighter cover, but their counterpart Seafires operated all day without pause. As soon as enemy aircraft were expected, the Seafires took to the air. Weather conditions were surprisingly severe and a rough sea made it very hard to land on the carrier decks. Some Seafires failed to stay on the flight deck and went overboard. These landing accidents contributed to a total loss of sixty Seafires in five days.

Spitfires flew right through the Italian campaign, continually worrying German troops. One of their ploys when attacking road convoys on the retreat in Italy was to go for the front and rear vehicles—thus making progress and escape impossible for the rest. Three months was the figure cited as the life-span for Spitfire and pilot alike: an indication of the nature of this campaign. Spitfire squadrons particularly involved in Italy were Nos 72 and 145.

72 Squadron Spitfires were also selected to support the invasion of southern France by French and American troops. When it became clear that enemy defence was weak, the squadron went back to Italy, where they were still badly needed. On 31 August 1944, they successfully attacked an enemy force of parked tanks, and on 3 September, their C.O., subsequently the famous test pilot, Neville Duke, destroyed two Me 109s. 145 Squadron watched the advance of the Eighth Army ripping through the vaunted Gothic Line.

An interesting sidelight was when a reconnaissance Spitfire, normally much too fast to be caught by the enemy, suddenly found a *jet* fighter on its tail, but succeeded in eluding it in the southern German Alps. On 18 October 1944, a Spitfire Mk IX had the honour of being the first R.A.F. aircraft to land again in Greece.

Harry Broadhurst and the Desert Air Force

Harry Broadhurst—then and now

In early June 1940, Harry Broadhurst was posted to Coltishall as a Wing Commander to command this new fighter station. He arrived to find no squadrons, only a 'Works and Bricks' section who were still building Coltishall. While he was there, he sighted an Air Ministry signal asking for a Wing Commander for immediate duty in France. 'Broady' volunteered. His A.O.C., Air Vice Marshal Leigh Mallory, expressed surprise that Broadhurst should wish to move so soon (a couple of days in fact) after joining 12 Group on promotion. Harry replied that he had no aeroplanes and nothing to command except some building operatives, so could he please go to France.

He duly arrived at Lille to find total chaos. Destroyed aircraft—British and French—littered the airfield. The British pilots and ground crews were in great heart, and determined to go on fighting while they had anything to fly.

With the German advance threatening the aerodrome, the squadrons retired to Merville, from whence they were ordered back to England. To Harry's delight Leigh Mallory gave him command of Wittering, near Stamford, with its Hurricanes. During the Battle of Britain, Broadhurst led the other 12 Group Wing, from Wittering. He had the same problems I had (with the Duxford Wing)—usually being called too late by 11 Group and told to patrol in the wrong place.

Throughout 1941, Group Captain Broadhurst had a highly successful fighting career. Although station commander at Hornchurch (Essex) he frequently led the Spitfire Wing. In 1942 he found time from his staff duties as Air Commodore to fire his guns. Eventually, in 1943, he found himself in North Africa, as an Air Vice Marshal in operational command of the Western Desert Air Force, with headquarters at Tripoli.

Broadhurst was the first World War II RAF officer to have reached this rank. He had gained rapid promotion through sheer ability and hard won experience in action; in France during her final hour; in Britain dependent on the Hurricane and Spitfire for survival; in operations over France in 1941 after the German tide had ebbed from the English shores; Dieppe in 1942; and now North Africa.

He knew what air superiority was all about; he talked the same language as his wing commanders and their pilots, some of whom had flown alongside him in battle. He could still lead them in the air if he decided to do so.

He had arrived in Africa at exactly the right time. Montgomery's Eighth Army had driven Rommel's Afrika Korps from Alamein back to Tunisia. General Le Clercq had brought his French army from Lake Chad in the south; the British First Army with our American allies were pressing in from Algeria. The Germans were caught in the area bounded by the Bay of Tunis. The sea was behind them, the Allies all round. We controlled the air overhead. Broadhurst was the sole air commander in North Africa who completely understood the way to use this air power. Of such is confidence bred.

Le Clercq's advance was being resisted by the German 21st Panzers. Broadhurst sent Billy Burton's wing, equipped with Hurricane IIds (two 40-mm cannons). Wing Commander Burton reported total success, adding: 'We must have hit the NAAFI because I came back with my air filter full of razor blades.'

Burton was an outstanding officer by any standards. He commanded 616 Squadron at Tangmere in 1941 when I had the Wing there; as a cadet at Cranwell before the war, he had won the Sword of Honour; he was typical of the best type of Englishman. He died in 1943 returning to North Africa from leave in England, when the aeroplane in which he was a passenger was shot down in the Bay of Biscay.

The Hurricane IId was a fine aiming platform, as Denys Gillam points out, but it proved disastrous against Panzers in lager. The IId required a long, low, straight run-in. The Panzers, when they were encamped and stationary (in lager), could depress their 88-mm guns and shoot accurately at the steadily approaching target which the IId presented.

Billy Burton and his pilots learned that lesson just once when nearly all got shot down. Some, including Burton, walked back to the British lines with blankets round them, hoping they looked like Arabs!

Rommel's Afrika Korps was being supplied with fuel and ammunition by the large Junkers 52 and Messerschmitt transports. These flew low across the Bay of Tunis and past Cap Bon. The Germans used to put up a high cover of fighters which was picked up by the Allied radar while the low flying transports evaded it. Broadhurst got the message at once; he had met it during the Battle of Britain. Spitfire IXs dealt with the fighters; Hurricanes and others caught the transports at low level. The enemy were annihilated. In one day, twenty-three out of twenty-five large transports were destroyed. This was the end. The remnants of the Luftwaffe, mainly fighters, which had any fuel flew out to Sicily. The Afrika Korps surrendered.

There was an interesting side-light to the introduction of the Spitfire IX to the Western Desert. Initially, it was fitted with a large air filter to stop the sand destroying the engine. The filter was in fact enormous and considerably reduced the aeroplane's performance. Rather like the inspired adaptation of the Spitfire V to high altitude against German reconnaissance aircraft over Alexandria, a solution was found. The sand problem occurred only on the ground with fast-turning propellers during run-up and take-off. So they fitted an air filter—jettisonable by parachute immediately after take-off—which enabled the Spitfire to become its immaculate self in the air.

Broadhurst moved his H.Q. to Malta ready for the follow-up invasion of Sicily and Italy— what Churchill called the 'soft under-belly of Europe'. Hurricanes and Spitfires had supported the Eighth Army all the way from Alamein; others had kept the sky clear for the First Army and our American allies from the landing at Algiers and their advance eastwards. Now they were together in Tunis for the grand finale. Soon they would depart for Malta which they had saved in 1942. Some would go on to Sicily and Italy, some back to England—and finally back to the sky over France, a hunting ground familiar to both Hurricane and Spitfire and not a few of their pilots. Harry Broadhurst would lead them across Europe in command of the Second Tactical Air Force.

Fighting up Italy by 'Cocky' Dundas

'Cocky' Dundas—then and now

Malta, in June 1943, was an extraordinary sight. The highly-seasoned wings of the Desert Air Force, which had followed the Eighth Army all the way from Alamein, were joined up with the rather more white-kneed wings which had been supporting the First Army in Tunisia. The island was crawling with aircraft, and a number of rough characters who would have been familiar to the author of this book, were making the best of enjoying the benefits of living in buildings instead of tents, and an abundance of bars in which to renew old acquaintanceships.

I was wing leader of 324 Wing, now five squadrons with a Wing Commander leading it and a Group Captain in command, which had been operating over Tunisia throughout the winter and spring campaign. 'Sheep' Gilroy commanded the wing.

Every day, and often twice or three times a day, we flew off in wing strength across the sixty miles of sea to sweep over Sicily, with two or three squadrons of light or medium bombers below us. The object, I believe, was primarily to get the enemy fighters up and out of the way before the landings started. And that object was to a large extent achieved. The Spitfire was performing in its classic role, and the author would have felt perfectly at home in my cockpit as we climbed, covering half the sky in our finger-four formations, breaking up when the clashes came, to rejoin again afterwards as best we could. It all went pretty well, though it was hard going at times, with plenty of shooting and a fair number of casualties. My wing claimed more than sixty enemy aircraft destroyed in that short, sharp warm-up campaign before we actually landed on 'D-Day' plus one at Capo Pachino, on an 800-yard dust strip.

In Sicily, we all lived in tented camps around our dusty airstrips, being eaten by flies and mosquitoes. Whenever a squadron or a flight taxied out for take-off, or taxied in again, our Spitfires were smothered in thick brown dust-clouds. Our operations consisted of escorting the day bombers as they attacked enemy supply lines north of the battle and of patrolling the bomb-line to intercept any German or Italian bombers which might seek to enter the fray. There was, in fact, little enemy air activity, except at night.

When the Sicilian campaign was over, 324 Wing was seconded to American command and sent to an airstrip on the north coast of the island. It soon turned out that our role was to supply air support for the Salerno landings. It was exactly 175 miles from our landing strip to the centre of the beach-head. So every sortie involved using eighty-gallon long-range tanks as well as being air-borne for the best part of three hours. And we were doing two sorties most days.

It was not exactly what the Spitfire was designed for. Still less so—in my opinion at the time—was the role which we were next called upon to play by our American commander, Brigadier 'Shorty' Hawkins. The Salerno affair was not going well: the ground forces were holding on to the beach-head by the skin of their teeth. Hawkins came to see us and said that it would be a shot in the arm for the soldiers if we actually landed some Spitfires there instead of operating from far-away Sicily. I asked him politely just where he expected us to operate from, having regard to the fact that the Germans were still shelling the beach and the Allied ships in the Bay. He replied that a strip had been prepared parallel with the beach, ready for our occupation.

We went in, with two squadrons and a lot of misgivings. The misgivings were not allayed by the fact that there were two batteries of British 25-pounders operating in some olive groves which ran parallel to, and only a few paces from, our landing strip, and on the sea side of it. They were banging away absolutely non-stop, firing, of course, directly across our runway and its approaches. I calculated that there must be almost as much metal as fresh air in the sky through which we had to fly when landing and taking off. So I went along to find the senior gunner, a lieutenant colonel who appeared flabbergasted when I suggested that he might stop shooting whenever we were in the circuit. He kept on saying that his orders were to fire away non-stop. He found it hard to understand why I should make such a request. 'Certainly not,' he said 'Certainly not.

Who the hell ever heard of a Spitfire being shot down by a 25-pounder!' He returned with fresh enthusiasm to his bang-bangs, and I went back disconsolate to my Spitfires.

We ended up with most of the wing crammed on to that precarious beach-head. But for some reason which I have never understood, the German gunners put only a few rounds on to our strip and our own gunners never got us. Within two or three days the Germans had been pushed back out of range and that curious episode was over.

During the autumn of 1943 and the winter of 1943/44, the Spitfire's role in Italy was unexciting and unspectacular. The Luftwaffe had withdrawn its day fighters to other battle fronts. The Italian Air Force had ceased to exist. There was little to be done in the pure fighter role.

Other wings of Desert Air Force, equipped with Kittyhawks and Mustangs, were developing to a fine art the role of close support for the Allied armies, which were slogging their way forward across the endless obstacles presented by the nature of Italian terrain—rivers, narrow valleys, mountains, fortress towns. Those wings became an extension of the Eighth Army's heavy artillery and they learned to operate in a close and trusted partnership with the army—a partnership which was at the time, I believe, quite unique.

I personally learned how close that partnership was when, in January 1944, I was posted to Harry Broadhurst's staff at Advance Headquarters of Desert Air Force at Vasto, on the east coast of Italy. Army Advance Headquarters was at the same place. The two were totally integrated and indivisible. And I learned quite a lot at first hand about how the fighter-bombers worked, because 239 Wing was based just a couple of miles down the coast from our headquarters. I kept my Spitfire there and I spent a lot of time with their remarkable and redoubtable commander, Colonel Laurie Wilmot, who used to strap two 500-lb. bombs on to his Mustang for his almost daily work-outs across the bomb line. At that time, I often thanked my lucky stars that I was not engaged upon this activity which I regarded as an unnatural and hazardous occupation for a fighter pilot. Fortunately I could not see into the future.

In May 1944 I went back to the squadrons, taking over from our old friend Stan Turner as wing leader of 244 Wing. I stayed with 244 Wing until the end of the war, and for more than a year thereafter, much of the time as its commanding officer, succeeding Brian Kingcombe in that appointment in October 1944.

Very soon after I joined the Wing we were told that our Spitfires were to be equipped to carry bombs. I cannot be certain that we were the first Spitfires to be cast in the role of fighter-bombers, but I believe we may have been.

For a few weeks we were given simple targets on which to cut our teeth—bridges and road junctions on the supply routes in central Italy. We learned to use our gun-sights as bomb-sights and quite quickly became adept at planting our bombs with reasonable accuracy. It was far from an exact science. You just got the feel of the thing—the angle of dive, the pull-through, the precise *moment-juste* for pressing the buttons and releasing the bomb.

By July 1944 we were ready for promotion to the role of close support. The Eighth Army was hammering away at the Gothic Line. We moved over to the east coast, and from then until the winter lull (winter that year in Italy was hard and wet and cold) we were using our Spitfires day in and day out to attack opportunity targets, often a few hundred yards in front of our ground forces.

All the time we were flying at fairly low altitudes—seldom above 8,000 feet before the bomb dive—and usually in a clear sky. The Germans had packed the area behind their lines with flak. As we ran into our targets we were subjected to a barrage of 88-mm fire. As we dived we went through a curtain of Bofors. When we strafed, we were met by machine-guns. The Germans believed in using plenty of tracer. So one could never imagine they were not there! It was hot work and we had quite a lot of casualties.

At an early stage in the activity I decided that maximum manoeuvrability was a top priority. I had the curved wing-tips cut off my Spitfire, so that they were squared away just outside the ailerons. This, of course, reduced the lift, which was a disadvantage both in taking off fully loaded from a short strip and in landing back on it again. But it gave me lightness of handling in the dive and in jinking through the flak when coming out at low level.

During the winter of 1944/45 the Allied advance was halted at the River Senio on the east coast. The weather was foul. Often cloud was too low for bombing and when air support was needed we could not always provide it in the conventional way. One day, when a section of the line was under pressure, the army called for support, but cloud base was down to about 1,000 feet—no good at all for dive bombing. My five squadrons were sitting on the ground, apparently useless. After consultations on the field telephone with one of the Desert Air Force ground controllers in a forward observation post, I took off with a squadron, having arranged that our artillery should put down a line of smoke shells where they needed support, just in front of our own troops. It worked beautifully. As soon as we were overhead and in contact with the observation post, a thin white line of smoke was laid down and we swept in, twelve Spitfires in line abreast, with cannons and machine-guns firing.

The final battle started early in April, with the crossing of the Senio. Several wings of Spitfires were engaged in constant air support. A measure of the confidence which had grown up between us and the army may be found in the fact that we were asked to strafe the north bank of the Senio—a narrow river, not more than twenty yards across at any point, though with high flood banking—while our own troops were dug into the south bank.

Hundreds of tanks and armoured vehicles, thousands of supply vehicles, and scores of coastal and river craft were destroyed by Spitfires during that last three weeks of war in Italy, when the German divisions were driven back over the Po and into the Alps. We flew from dawn until dusk—take-off, bomb, strafe, fly home, refuel and re-arm, take-off again. It was a frenetic period. The end was in sight but the battle was more furious than ever. I had had a special bomb-rack designed which enabled me to carry two bombs side by side under my Spitfire. I think we were all— particularly those of us who had been at it since early 1940 —a little dotty by this time. When my second-in-command was killed about a week after the offensive started, my Italian servant hid my flying boots, in the hope that this would prevent me from flying! When that ruse was unsuccessful he took to calling me in the morning with a tumbler of Marsala mixed with raw egg, presumably with a view to rendering me incapable.

On V-day we landed at Treviso, and I received the signal to say that hostilities were over. You may imagine what went on in the mess that night. The celebrations were marred, however, by the receipt, at a late hour, of an instruction to put a patrol up at dawn to cover the northward passage through the Alps of some railway trains. The mystery of what was in those trains and why they needed an escort is only exceeded by the mystery of how I and eleven other bleary-eyed pilots, specially selected by me for their proven ability to fly in the face of excessive alcoholic intake, survived the patrol. It was a case of the blind leading the blind. But once more our Spitfires carried us through.

Photographic reconnaissance

The pilots of the Photographic Reconnaissance made a tremendous contribution to the conduct and ultimate winning of the war. The names of these pilots, some of them highly decorated— like Adrian Warburton, D.S.O., D.F.C., the greatest of them all—are unknown outside the Royal Air Force. Yet their courage was equal to the best.

The Spitfire gave these pilots what they needed to carry out their unique and lonely job. Stripped of its guns, radio, and every last bit of unneeded weight, painted sky-blue, and polished to an immaculate finish, the P.R.U. Spitfire could fly higher and faster than any Me 109, and way beyond interference from anti-aircraft fire. Its weapons were cameras; its defence, speed.

That wise and far-seeing Commander-in-Chief of Fighter Command, Lord Dowding, had early recognized the importance of photo-reconnaissance. Months before the Battle of Britain, the presiding genius (civilian Sidney Cotton) behind the P.R. conception had spoken to Dowding and explained why the P.R. Spitfire was essential. At the end of the conversation, Dowding, decisive as ever, said: 'You will have two of my precious Spitfires tomorrow morning.'

The high-flying Spitfires roamed far and wide over enemy-occupied territory. The Admiralty was especially interested in the P.R.U. The Royal Navy needed to know the whereabouts of the big German ships, so as to intercept them before they could get out into the Atlantic and cause havoc amongst our convoys. A young pilot Michael Suckling found the *Bismarck* in a Norwegian fjord.

Wing Commander Geoffrey Tuttle, D.F.C., was the first C.O. of the P.R.U. He retired from the Royal Air Force as Air Marshal Sir Geoffrey. The P.R.U. pilots not only flew high, they flew low—and very low sometimes, to identify certain heavily protected enemy targets. Many were lost on such missions.

The Spitfire continued in its P.R. role until the end of the war; although half-way through, the twin-engined, two-seater, Mosquito came increasingly into the picture in this capacity.

More on the P.R. story can be found in Constance Babington Smith's superb book *Evidence in Camera*. The author served as a photographic interpreter in the P.R.U.

I thought the following verses, written by a P.R.U. pilot, should conclude this account.

Unidentified

This is the tale of the Gremlins
   Told by the P.R.U.
At Benson and Wick and St. Eval—
   And believe me, you slobs, it's true.

When you're seven miles up in the heavens,
   (That's a hell of a lonely spot)
And it's fifty degrees below zero
   Which isn't exactly hot.

When you're frozen blue like your Spitfire
   And you're scared a mosquito pink,
When you're thousands of miles from nowhere
   And there's nothing below but the drink—

It's then you will see the Gremlins,
   Green and gamboge and gold,
Male and female and neuter,
   Gremlins both young and old.

It's no good trying to dodge them,
   The lessons you learnt on the Link
Won't help you evade a Gremlin
   Though you boost and you dive and you jink.

White ones will wiggle your wingtips,
   Male ones will muddle your maps,
Green ones will guzzle your Glycol,
   Females will flutter your flaps.

Pink ones will perch on your perspex,
   And dance pirouettes on your prop;
There's a spherical middle-aged Gremlin
   Who'll spin on your stick like a top.

They'll freeze up your camera shutters,
   They'll bite through your aileron wires,
They'll bend and they'll break and they'll batter,
   They'll insert toasting forks in your tyres.

That is the tale of the Gremlins,
   Told by the P.R.U.,
(P)retty (R)uddy (U)nlikely to many,
   But fact, none the less, to the few.

PR Spitfire Mark XI

Striking into Europe

By 1943, the Allies were on the offensive all over Europe. Everyone knew that the invasion of northern France was inevitable. Before it came, both Spitfires and Hurricanes softened up the enemy in many places and many ways. One of the more unusual was by night offensive patrols. It is worth quoting an official report of one such sortie:

'I'm afraid the dangers and hazards of flying on night offensive patrols have been rather exaggerated. Certainly the average intruder pilot is not the cat-eyed, carrot-eating killer that the Press sometimes makes him out to be. Most of us night fighters are too fond of our mornings in bed to go flying in the daytime. Give me a moonlight night and my old Hurricane, and you can have your Spitfires and dawn readiness! We've no formation flying to worry about, and no bombers to escort. In fact, nothing to do but amuse ourselves once we've crossed the French coast.

'I must admit that those miles of Channel with only one engine brings mixed thoughts, and one can't help listening to every little beat of the old Merlin, as the English coast disappears in the darkness. I always get a feeling of relief and excitement as I cross the French coast and turn on the reflector sight, knowing that anything I see then I can take a crack at. We have to keep our eyes skinned the whole time, and occasionally glance at the compass and clock. As the minutes go by and we approach the Hun aerodrome, we look eagerly for the flare paths. More often than not, we are disappointed. The flare path is switched off as soon as we arrive, and up come the searchlights and flak. But if you're lucky, it's a piece of cake.

'The other night I saw the Jerries when I was still some distance away. They were flying round at about 2,000 feet. I chose the nearest and followed him round. He was batting along at about 200 miles an hour, but I soon caught him, and got him beautifully lined up in my sights before letting him have it.

'The effect of our four cannon is incredible after the eight machine-guns I had previously been used to. Scarcely had I pressed the button when a cluster of flashes appeared on the bomber and a spurt of dark red flame came from its starboard engine. The whole thing seemed to fold up then and fall out of the sky. I turned steeply to watch it crash and as I did so I saw another Hun about a mile away, coming straight for me. In half a minute he was in my sights, and a second later his port petrol tank was blazing. I gave him another short burst for luck and then flew beside him.

'It was just like watching a film. A moment before he hit the ground, I could see trees and houses lit up by the dark red flare from the burning machine. Suddenly there was a terrific sheet of flame, and little bits of burning Heinkel flew in all directions.

'I flew straight back to the aerodrome to find another. Unfortunately all the lights had been switched off, and though I circled for some time I found nothing. So I cracked off for home.

Previous pages; top:
Spitfires on mission shortly
before D-Day and (below)
small section of the D-Day
armada

Below: Seafire in Normandy,
July 1944

I looked back once and could still see the two searchlights trying vainly to find me. On the way back I spotted a train. They're easy to see in the moonlight, as the trail of steam shows up nicely against the dark background. I made sure it was a goods train before attacking the engine, which I left enveloped in a cloud of steam. My squadron has rather specialized in this train-wrecking racket. During the April/May full moon, we blew up seventeen engines for certain, and probably several others.

'Well, when your petrol and ammunition are nearly gone, you are faced with the old Channel again. If you've got something, as I had that night, you leave the enemy territory with a sort of guilty conscience; not for what you've done, but somehow you feel they've got it in for you, and that everyone's going to shoot at you. It's a sort of nervous reaction I suppose. The whole thing seems too easy to be true. Ten to one there's no Hun within shooting distance, and the ground defences are quiet. That makes it all the worse, and I generally weave about till I'm half-way back across the Channel. If you've done nothing, of course, you don't get this feeling, as you're still looking for something at which to empty your ammunition—trains inland and barges and ships on the coast. We've had some of these recently, too.

'Out over the Channel, you can hear your ground station calling the other aircraft of the squadron, and you count the minutes and look eagerly for the coast. Often it seems to take so long coming back that you feel the compass is wrong. At last, in the distance, you see the flashing beacon, and soon you are taxiing into your dispersal point. I dread the look of disappointment on my mechanic's face if my guns are unfired. But if the rubber covers have been shot off, I've scarcely time to stop my engine before I am surrounded by the boys asking what luck I've

had. Then comes the best part of the whole trip—a cup of tea and a really good line-shooting session!

'My whole squadron, both ground crews and pilots, are as keen as mustard, and I must say they've put up a terrific show. Since 1 April, the squadron has destroyed eleven aircraft for certain and probably three more, apart from the seventeen trains and the odd boat.'

So to 1944. Spitfire Mk IXs were to be in action for D-Day. Bomb adaptation carriers were added, as well as the other amendments. Spitfires were now bombers as well. 411 (R.C.A.F.) Squadron had the ill-luck to lose their commanding officer during one of these bombing raids. It happened on 19 May 1944 as he took his Spitfire towards the target at Hazebrouck. The bomb he was carrying received a direct hit from enemy flak.

Radar stations in the Pas de Calais zone were intentionally not bombed, because they would be wanted by the Allies to give the Germans information of a dummy invasion there.

D-Day—6th June. As the Allied troops hit the beach-heads, more Spitfire squadrons gave them protective cover. The Allied Expeditionary Air Force clocked up the phenomenal sortie total of 14,674 in that day. One Canadian pilot, shot down into the Channel on D−1 Day, had a grandstand view of the Armada from a dinghy as he sat forty-two hours waiting to be rescued. Enemy fighter interceptors seemed to be strangely missing most of the time on D-Day itself and D+1. Pilot Officer Kidd, a Canadian of 602 Squadron, may well have been the first Allied pilot to come down in France—inadvertently. He was forced to land in the American section of the minute beach-head.

Air operations inevitably expanded. By D+4, 144 Wing of R.C.A.F. Squadrons 441, 442, and 443 was in full operation and before the end of June, thirty Spitfire squadrons were based inside the Allied lines.

Back on the mainland of Europe: RAF and Dominion pilots on airstrip in Normandy

On 17 July, 602 Squadron happened to see and attack a trio of German vehicles on a local road. The car tipped over. Unknown to them, one of the passengers was Field Marshal Rommel and his skull was fractured.

Spitfires made many cannon attacks on armour during the fight for Caen. After the crucial early battles in Normandy, a quantity of Spitfires was spared for return to Britain.

Shortly after D-Day Hitler launched his first secret weapon against Britain. It took the form of a short, pilotless aeroplane which travelled between 300 and 400 m.p.h. and had a ton of high-explosive in its nose; the V-1. The first of them fell on England on 13 June. Thousands followed. Spitfires were among the fighters which tried to prevent the weapons reaching their destinations. Shooting at them from close range could be fatal. On 23 June, one Spitfire pilot adopted his own approach. He flew beside the V-1, edged nearer until the wing of the Spitfire was lodged beneath that of the V-1 and then he tilted his wing—tipping the V-1 out of control to the ground safely out of harm's way.

In September Spitfires flew to assist in the ill-fated Arnhem airborne landings. But with opposition in the air disappearing, Spitfires were employed increasingly in ground attack.

6 October 1944 saw a significant encounter when 401 (R.C.A.F.) Squadron ran into a Me 262 jet over the Nijmegen locality. The jet was 500 feet lower down, so the Canadian leader utilized this advantage in attacking. The Me 262 was destroyed, but the arrival of the jet opened a new age.

After the V-1, the V-2, a far more formidable weapon. These were rockets, and travelled far faster than the V-1s, and thus could not be destroyed in the air. They also carried more explosive. To give an idea of the havoc of these new terror weapons, the one which fell on 25 November scored a direct hit on Woolworth's store in New Cross, London: 160 people were killed and 135 injured.

Intelligence thought that the launch area for the V-2s was somewhere near The Hague in Holland. Spitfire Mk XVIs of 602 and 453 (R.C.A.F.) Squadrons went for suspected sites. On Christmas Eve, Spitfires attacked this same stores-and-launch region.

On Christmas Day, Lieutenant J. J. Boyle of 411 (R.C.A.F.) Squadron despatched two more Me 262 jets, which were reckoned rapid but less manoeuvrable than his own Spitfire Mk IX. This was followed by a last throw by the Luftwaffe in 1945. They managed to destroy a lot of Spitfires on the ground, but their own losses proved appalling—and Allied air attacks on aircraft and component factories made replacements impossible. Even as late in the European operations as 30 April 1945, Spitfires were slogging it out with FW 190s and Me 109s. But only for one more week. Then came victory in Europe.

The final thrust by 'Johnnie' Johnson

Johnnie Johnson—then and now

For some time, the planning for the invasion of Normandy had been in full swing at Fighter Command, but this Command, with its underground concrete operations rooms, its permanent communications and permanent airfields, was a static, defensive organization. Its squadrons could move, but not its essential being. Therefore it had been decided that, although the defence of Britain—the base for the invasion—should remain Fighter Command's responsibility, the fighters that would maintain air supremacy over and beyond the Normandy beaches must belong to a more flexible organization geared to the needs of the invading armies. The new force had to be mobile. It had to be able to build airfields, lay communications, establish its own radar system, and move ever forward. Moreover, our Spitfires would, in future, be dual purpose. First, when there was air opposition in the form of enemy fighters, we would carry on with the usual business of gaining air superiority over the armies below.

Secondly, when there was no opposition in the air, we were instructed to fit bombs onto our Spitfires and get on with the business of providing close air support for the army—that is, the beating up of enemy strong-points, gun positions, tanks, armoured cars, and the like.

At this time the Spitfire IX was the best air fighter in the world. In my view it was not suitable for beating-up the ground targets I have described, because its Merlin engine was cooled by a liquid called Glycol, which was held in a small tank just below the propeller. This Glycol tank and the radiator were always exposed to ground fire, at which the Germans were very adept. A single machine-gun bullet through either the radiator or the Glycol tank meant that the engine caught fire or seized up

within a matter of a very few minutes. After four years of air fighting, and still remaining sound in wind and limb, the prospect of being shot down by a few rounds fired by some half-baked Kraut gunner did not appeal to me in the least!

The first time I saw my lean and graceful Spitfire with two 500-lb. bombs hanging beneath its slender wings, it seemed to me that she was intolerably burdened, and that the ugly blunt bombs were a basic contradiction of all the beauty and symmetry of the aircraft. It was like seeing a beautiful racehorse harnessed to a farm cart.

Looking back, I think I was unduly sensitive about this ground attack business. I thought it was one thing for a specially designed ground attack aeroplane, like the German Stuka, to be employed on dive-bombing and ground strafing, but it was quite another matter to force this delicate and sensitive aeroplane into a steep dive, to aim it at the target, and release your bombs at about the same time as you pulled out of the dive. In fact it seemed all very much a hit and miss affair, although some pilots became very accurate and seemed actually to enjoy this type of work.

The other reason why I did not like our ground attack role was that for the last few years I had been wholly engaged in air fighting. We had always flown at medium and high altitudes and we had been taught, through sheer necessity, to twist our necks every few seconds to keep a sharp look-out for the Hun in the sun. But when we were flying in the ground attack role we had to concentrate on the navigation, and had to keep peering down at the ground to make sure of our exact position; and, of course, while we were doing this we could not pay any attention to what was going on behind. We had so far spent the entire war looking behind. Now we looked downwards and forwards all the time. And who wanted to be concentrating for several minutes on navigation and the identification of difficult ground targets when Adolf Galland and his Messerschmitts or Mantoni and his Focke-Wulf 190s were queuing up behind to 'bounce' your Spitfire from the sun?

The Tactical Air Forces taking part in the invasion of Normandy, on 6 June 1944 were, by present-day standards, colossal. The fighter-bombers, medium bombers, transport aeroplanes, artillery observation aeroplanes, and tactical reconnaissance aeroplanes, totalled more than 9,000 aircraft. In addition to these were the thousands of strategic bombers. These air forces were directed from a combined control centre at Uxbridge where, less than four years before when the Battle of Britain had reached its height, the New Zealand commander of 11 Group, Keith Park, told Winston Churchill that his group had no fighter squadrons in reserve.

On the early morning of this day I led my Canadian Wing of three squadrons across the choppy, grey Channel to patrol the eastern flank of the assault. The visibility was fair, about five miles, but the cloud base was down to around 2,000 feet, which meant that a great many aeroplanes were compressed into a small air space. I called the wing leader of the Spitfires we were about to relieve and told him we were on our patrol line. Had he seen any enemy fighters? 'Not a bloody thing,' he replied, 'but there are plenty of ours milling about, and the flak is pretty hot.' I called the fighter direction ship below and asked if there were any plots of German formations. The controller came back with the guarded reply that for the moment he had nothing for me.

We swept parallel to the coast beneath the leaden sky, and I positioned the Wing a few hundred yards off-shore so that the enemy gunners, for whom we always had the utmost respect, could not range on our Spitfires. We were forced down to a low altitude by intermittent cloud.

The air space became dangerously crowded as fighters, fighter-bombers, light bombers, medium bombers, reconnaissance aeroplanes, and gun spotters twisted and turned above the choppy sea. The danger was not from the Luftwaffe, but from a mid-air collision.

Four times that day we made our way across the Channel and did not see a German aeroplane. We were bitterly disappointed with the Luftwaffe's failure to make an appearance on this day—one of the most momentous in the long and turbulent history of Europe. They were, of course, heavily engaged in other theatres, particularly on the eastern front against the Russians. Long after the war Alf Galland told us that on Hitler's instructions many German fighter squadrons had been withdrawn to the homeland because Hitler thought it was better for the German people to see British or American bombers brought down over Germany. This, of course, was a foolish decision, as the bombers should have been met as far forward as possible.

A few days later we moved into France and established ourselves at an airfield within the beachhead. The following months, until the Germans were defeated in the spring of 1945, were the most interesting and exciting of all the war years. For, at last, we were getting somewhere. In supporting the army we were on the move, and to all of us it seemed as though we were now playing a bigger and more decisive part in the war. The morale of my Canadian fighter Wing was very high. We knew we were flying the best fighter in the world. Also our morale was helped by the great reception we received from the French people, in all walks of life, who had suffered the Germans for more than four long years and seemed to understand that the invasion could not have taken place before this time because of the long years of build-up and preparation.

The Luftwaffe had to divide its attention between the 1,500-mile long Russian front, the Mediterranean, the bombing of Britain, the Atlantic shipping routes, and the defence of Germany. However, one of the Luftwaffe's great qualities was its flexibility, and squadrons were often moved thousands of miles to reinforce a threatened position. So it was that a few weeks after we had established ourselves in Normandy the Luftwaffe switched hundreds of fighters and fighter-bombers from Germany to France where they carried out low-flying attacks against Allied forward troops and armour. The enemy flew in smaller numbers than before, for two reasons: first, they wanted to keep down the number of aeroplanes flying from one airfield, and secondly, the greater speeds and altitudes of the latest fighters meant wider turning circles and less manoeuvrability. Large formations to punch holes in the mass daylight raids were still wanted for defensive purposes, but the close and swift skirmishes over Normandy made it impossible for a leader to handle more than a dozen fighters. We, too, found that Wing fighting was on the way out, as thirty-six aircraft were now too unwieldly and too conspicuous. I flew once or twice each day, leading the various squadrons in turn so that I did not lose my intimate association with them.

Our Spitfire IXs were now fitted with the latest gyroscopic gunsights which automatically computed the amount of deflection one should allow when attacking a German aeroplane. A fighter pilot simply aimed the guns by flying his Spitfire so that the cross bisected the target—the range was ideal when the surrounding 'diamonds' embraced the silhouette of his opponent. Some pilots obtained remarkable results with this device, but I found that I spent too long with my head in the office as it were, peering into the sight and not paying enough attention to my tail. I preferred the old-fashioned simple reflector sight, which I kept installed in my personal Spitfire until the war was over.

After the Luftwaffe had reinforced the

Normandy sector, we met and fought their 109s and 190s daily over the Normandy countryside. Whenever the weather permitted they were active over the battle area, and we ranged far to the south so as to cut them off before they could attack our ground troops. Apart from their leaders, their pilots seemed a poor, ill-trained lot who bore little resemblance to the veterans we had fought three or four years ago. Consequently the 109 gave us little trouble in our versatile Spitfire IXs, and indeed on one occasion one of my squadron commanders, Wally McLeod, shot down two Focke-Wulf 190s with only thirteen rounds from each of his two cannon. Each gun carried a total of 120 rounds so that McLeod had used only about one tenth of his ammunition. It was a remarkable display of both flying and shooting skill and, as far as I know, the performance was never equalled. Another squadron commander, Tommy Brannagan, brought off a resounding and spectacular victory against the 190s. Leading his squadron of twelve Spitfires into an equal number of Focke-Wulf 190s, Tommy's tactics were so successful that only two of the enemy managed to get away. Ten 190s was a record to be proud of, especially as our only casualty was an enemy cannon shell in the wing of a Spitfire.

Eventually our ground forces broke out of the Normandy beachhead and advanced towards Paris. Soon afterwards my Canadian Wing moved in that direction and for a few days we were based only a few miles from the French capital. My Group Captain, Bill McBrian, suggested an evening in Paris and after doing the rounds we eventually repaired to the Ritz and decided to have a final glass of champagne on the balcony of our suite overlooking the Place van Dam. As we took our seats in the moonlight on the balcony, we were just in time to see Bill's official Humber staff car being driven slowly out of the square by a group of young Frenchmen in berets, who waved to us gaily and then disappeared. The staff car was never seen again. Years afterwards I received an invoice from some civil servant for half the estimated cost of the vehicle, together with the request that I was to send off my cheque immediately. I replied that I could not possibly be held responsible, as I was merely acting on the orders of my superior officer, Group Captain McBrian.

Meanwhile, back in Canada, Bill also received a similar invoice, but he did not even take the trouble to answer and tell them what to do with it!

When we were in the Brussels area in the autumn of 1944, our trusty Spitfire IXs were taken away and we were re-equipped with the Spitfire XVI, which was basically the same as the Spitfire IX except that it was fitted with an American-built Merlin 66 engine.

Somehow or other the Americans, when building the Merlin engine under licence in the States, had put the wrong metal in the big ends. As a result of this a considerable number of these Spitfire XVIs seized up and

The jet age arrived with a new formidable opponent for the Spitfire—the Me 262 (inset). The USAF Mustang (extreme right, at the top of the picture) is in process of destroying an Me 262. Photo taken from gun camera of another Mustang

caught fire in the air. For several weeks we were puzzled as to why we were losing so many fighter pilots who would be seen to be flying serenely along one moment and then the next the engine would be in flames, the chap either going down or trying to bale out. Apparently we were not over any known flak belt, and we could only surmize that we had been flying over German flak and not seen it fired from the ground. But soon afterwards it was revealed that this particular batch of engines for the Spitfire XVI was faulty. Although I made the strongest representations to get back our old Spitfire IXs, this proved to be impossible and we had to make the most of an appalling job, and go on flying the faulty Spitfire XVIs, which cost the Wing a large number of casualties.

To make matters worse for us in our wretched Spitfire XVIs, with the approach of the war's fifth winter the Germans brought into service their first jet aeroplanes. The best of these was the twin-engined Messerschmitt 262, which was developed both as a bomber and a fighter because everyone in the Luftwaffe wanted this outstanding machine. The bomber protagonists wanted it because its speed of well over 500 m.p.h. and the great altitude at which it could fly, made it ideal for attacking Britain's crowded airfields. The fighter advocates, led by Alf Galland, wanted it to stop the daylight raids. When Hitler saw the jet he called it 'the blitz bomber'.

But Galland fought hard for the new and outstanding jet, and somehow got a few 262s together to prove them in combat. He thought that if they were successful the Fuhrer might change his mind. Soon this new jet fighter with its four 30-mm cannon, began destroying our high-flying Mosquito bombers which had long roamed free over Germany. Whenever we fighter pilots came across a 262 we could not catch it because of its remarkable speed and climb. In fact suddenly the jet age had arrived, and now our piston-engine fighters were outmoded and obsolete. Realizing that we could not tackle the jets once they were in the air we carried out frequent strafing attacks against their airfields to smash the 262s on the ground. But these attacks were costly. The thick and accurate flak brought down many Spitfires and Tempests. Then we tried patrols near the enemy airfields but beyond their flak belts to hit the 262s as they took off or came in to land. It was only like this that we were able to prevent the relatively small number of Me 262 fighters from becoming dangerous. Meanwhile, in order to counter the Me 262, the R.A.F. introduced its first squadron of Meteor IIIs, also a twin-engined jet fighter.

They were based near Brussels, but the performance of the Meteor III did not approach that of the Me 262. Their poor climb and moderate range made them totally unsuitable for combat. After more powerful engines were fitted to the Meteors they did in fact carry out some ground attacks and strafing, but they never destroyed an enemy aeroplane in the air over Europe. I think that is the measure of the difference between the two jets. The Meteor IIIs were really put in to the front line for prestige.

On 1 January 1945 the Luftwaffe mounted its last major attack of the war, when some 800 fighters and fighter-bombers crossed the Rhine. Flying very low in four great waves, they were led and navigated by bombers who turned back near the Rhine. The fighter-bombers went on to attack thirteen British and four American airfields. The enemy achieved complete tactical surprise, perhaps not surprising as it was on New Year's day. Their cannons were already sounding over several airfields when the radar controller called up and ordered our fighters into the air.

On that day at Eindhoven, where the Royal Canadian Air Force fighter reconnaissance and Typhoon Wings were stationed, routine work was being carried out. The pilots of one squadron, the Toronto Squadron, were on their way to the airfield from their billets. Eight aircraft of another squadron were flying, and other pilots were sitting at their aircraft dispersal waiting for instructions. Suddenly at 9.20 in the morning two waves of 190s and 109s, together with some jet-propelled aircraft, filled the sky and carried out a series of persistent and well led strafing attacks which lasted for more than twenty minutes. As the Germans withdrew, the scene was one of devastation. Strangely enough, a friend of mine, Dean Nesbit, was just taking over the Typhoon Wing from another Canadian friend, Paul Davoud. When the attacks started the two Group Captains had leapt into a slit-trench. Now, as the Germans withdrew, they surveyed the mass of burning and damaged aircraft. Davoud said to Nesbit: 'Well, Dean, I guess it's all yours!'

Shortly afterwards I was promoted to take over the command of a British Spitfire 14 Wing and my days with the Canadians were over. It was the spring of 1945, the war was almost over, and it was more than two years since I had first led the Canadians back at Kenley. Some of the more senior pilots had flown with me many times, and there existed between us that bond of comradeship that only those who have served and fought together are privileged to know.

13 THE BATTLE FOR ASIA
The war against Japan

The first Hurricanes arrived at Singapore in crates just after New Year's Day, 1942. They were in action against Japanese bombers on 20 January and shot down eight. The next day they ran into Zero fighters, which were a different kettle of fish and five Hurricanes were lost.

By early February the Hurricanes had been reduced to seven in Singapore and these retreated south-eastwards to Sumatra. Singapore fell that same month. On 15 February the projected invasion of Sumatra by the Japanese received a bloody nose. Hurricanes intercepted a sea-convoy on the way as well as destroying some Zero fighters at Banka Island. It was, however, only a temporary set-back. Ever retreating, the Hurricanes moved back to Java and by 18 February eighteen were left to defend Batavia. By 1 March they were twelve and on 7 March they had gone back to Bandoeng, where now only two remained. These were destroyed on the ground by the British.

The R.A.F. in Java were ably supported by the Dutch Java Air Force, who also had twenty-four Hurricanes. By the end of the campaign and before the Allied Forces withdrew, the Dutch had destroyed some thirty enemy aircraft for the loss of nearly all of their own Hurricanes.

Over in Burma the story at this stage was much the same. Thirty Hurricanes destined for Singapore had been stopped at Rangoon to help in its defence. By 11 February only half remained operational, and by the first week in March they numbered six. On 8 March Rangoon fell. Other Hurricanes in Burma operated from Mergui to the south. From there they heard that a number of Japanese aircraft had landed 200 miles further south. Ten Hurricanes and nine Blenheims found them and destroyed half of them on the ground as well as nine in the air.

Success was short lived, however, for the Japanese mounted a non-stop attack day and night on Mergui which wiped it out and most of the Hurricanes on it.

During the retreat from Burma Frank Carey, who had greatly distinguished himself in the Battle of Britain with 43 Squadron, led the Hurricanes. He had a colossal reputation at this time and estimates of his successes range as high as thirty enemy aircraft destroyed. On one occasion it is reported that just after take-off he found six Japanese Oscars on his tail. With an eye for terrain he dived towards a hill and pulled out very late with the result that one Oscar flew straight into the hillside. Frank was a great

Previous pages: Hurribomber attacking Japanese target in Burma. Above: Hurricane Mark II of China-British Squadron in dive. Below: two Hurricane Mark IIds in Burma

pilot. I asked him to write me a reminiscence about combat with the famous Japanese fighter, the Zero, at which I understood he was experienced. He replied that he had never seen a Zero except in a war museum.

After retreating from Burma the Hurricanes re-grouped in India and when the Japanese mounted an air-raid on Calcutta the Hurricanes inflicted heavy losses on them—such heavy losses that they did not repeat it. Throughout 1943 the fighter defences of India were greatly reinforced. By June there were sixteen squadrons of Hurricanes and from then on more appeared until in 1944 Spitfires and American Thunderbolts arrived.

The vast Northern Territories of Australia were quite obviously a gleam in the eye of the Japanese High Command. The enemy forces had got pretty near in their conquest of New Guinea. However, Spitfires had reached Australia in 1943 and equipped squadrons 54, 452, and 457. There were a few preliminary skirmishes with the Japanese in February and March and on 2 May a large force of Japanese bombers escorted by fighters appeared over Darwin.

Thirty-three Spitfires went off to meet them and battle was joined at 26,000 feet with the enemy losing this first round. The wing leader in the Port Darwin area was Clive 'Killer' Caldwell from Sydney. He had served in the Western Desert in the latter half of 1941 with considerable success. He returned to Australia in 1942 and first encountered the Japanese in the air on 2 March 1943. On this occasion he destroyed a Zeke as well as a torpedo bomber. He continued to knock them down on each encounter, the last one being on 20 August 1943.

The Spitfire Vs flown by the Australians were faster than their Zero adversaries, which was of course a great advantage. The Zero appears to have been a lightly built manoeuvrable fighter with a comparatively low wing loading and a radial engine. But it seems to have been unable to take heavy punishment from the 20-mm. cannons with which the Spitfire V was equipped.

Back in Burma the land battle was at a crucial stage. On 16 March 1944, the enemy cut the final land link to our troops up north and so set the scene for the siege of Imphal. There were six Hurricane squadrons there, and for the whole three months replenishment for the troops had to be from the air. The Hurricanes were ordered to break up any move against Imphal.

This is part of an official report on the siege:

'The tactical reconnaissance Hurricanes searched day by day for enemy movements and positions, delivering attacks as opportunities offered; owing both to the wild and rugged nature of the countryside, and to the ingenuity of the enemy in laying traps and in concealing himself, this was a task that called for a high degree of skill in both flying and observation. They spotted

I have found it impossible to get a first hand account from British Hurricane or Spitfire pilots who tangled with Japanese fighters in the Far East. I can do no better than quote the report of an Army officer.

In the fight for Arakan, Kohima, and Imphal, Brigadier M. R. Roberts gave an official ground-level view of an air battle between Spitfires and Zeros:

'On 10 February 1944, about eighty-plus Zeros and others came over and stooged around and then started to peel off by squadrons. I put on my tin hat and made for my command post, but as I was entering the slit I heard the high whine of

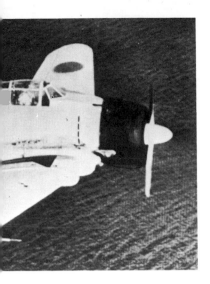

hotted up Spitfires. The battle took place right above my head and in twenty minutes I saw fifteen Japs go down. These were all that the air force actually claimed destroyed, but they put in fourteen as probable and twenty-three damaged.

'I saw one Jap Zero swoop down and I thought he was going to shoot us up, then he shot up again practically perpendicular, towering like a pheasant hit in the lungs—then he fell backwards and crashed.

'In view of the fact that after that battle I never saw more than three Jap aircraft at any one time, my view is that both the probables and the damaged were in fact destroyed.'

for artillery units, took photographs as required, passed information as to the location of our own forces, and dropped messages . . .

'No less valuable was the work of the ground attack Hurricanes, most versatile of aircraft. They performed an indispensable service in the early period of the Japanese offensive by their persistent attacks upon the forward Japanese lines of communication at a time when the enemy was making every effort to bring up his stores and armaments westwards. One squadron in particular came to specialize in what proved very remunerative attacks upon Japanese lorries on moonlight nights. At first the vehicles were easily detected by their headlights, but after two or three evenings they took to moving about without artificial illumination and the Hurricane pilots were thus compelled to seek their prey by selecting such well-known traffic lines as the Ye-U-Kelewa road and searching for lorries as they picked their way in the moonlight. When the perennial Japanese shortage of motor transport is taken into consideration, it will be realized how materially these attacks helped to blunt the offensive impetus of the enemy . . .

'Ground attack Hurricanes attacked locomotives and rolling stock . . . constantly searched the Chindwin for enemy rivercraft . . . and in May and June a total of at least fifteen enemy tanks were put out of commission by the Hurricanes.'

The Fourteenth Army began its north Burma offensive immediately before the monsoon broke, but even when the rains came, went on. Artillery mortars and four squadrons of Hurricanes collaborated in a neutralizing bombardment which helped the ground forces capture the aptly-named feature of Vital Corner on 2 November 1944.

Hurricanes flew on throughout the campaign. Two of them on patrol over Akyab on 2 January 1945 were able to report back from the signals of the locals that the enemy had left the island. In central Burma, Hurribombers destroyed five enemy bunkers while attacking a strongpoint at Gangaw, west of Mandalay. This aided the seizure of Myaukkon by the ground troops without fatal loss.

Down the Sittang and Irrawaddy, the same sort of air operations went on. The scent of victory was abroad. Hurricanes and other aircraft hit the earthworks of Fort Dufferin Castle. The city fell to our troops on 20 March, the very same date.

Across in the Pacific, Seafires were operating off H.M.S. *Implacable*, part of British Task Force 37. In July 1945, the Seafires undertook an offensive sweep when the aircraft carrier was a mere 130 miles from Tokyo itself. But then they received order to halt all air activities pending the execution of a special operation—Hiroshima.

EPILOGUE

I have endeavoured to write the story of the Spitfire and Hurricane. Although the book is finished, their story never will be. It involves too many people. Indeed this book is about people as well as aeroplanes and I am aware that I have left out many people. This was inevitable, and I know they will forgive me because that is their character.

It is thirty-four years since Squadron Leader John Gillan flew the first Hurricane delivered to his 111 Squadron from Edinburgh (Turnhouse) to London (Northolt) at an average speed of 407 m.p.h. Now the Hurricane, with its superlative and more famous successor and comrade-in-arms, the Spitfire, has become part of the history of the British people. Their names will ever be linked with those of their respective designers—Sidney Camm of the Hawker Hurricane and R. J. Mitchell of the Supermarine Spitfire. The latter is probably the most universally famous name in aeronautical history. As I have said before, in the dark days of the German domination of Europe, the word 'Spitfire' became synonymous with eventual freedom to the citizens of the occupied countries across the English Channel and the North Sea. It was a symbol that good would triumph over evil. In the breasts of the Luftwaffe bomber crews over England during the Battle of Britain it inspired fear. '*Achtung Schpitfeuer!*' their rear gunners would shout as a British fighter closed in. More often, it would be a Hurricane, for Hurricanes were more numerous in those days and in any case the Spitfires would usually be going for the Me 109s.

Peter Townsend, in his excellent book *Duel of Eagles*, refers to this perpetual '*Schpitfeuer* complex' of the Luftwaffe as 'Spitfire snobbery'. A splendid phrase. He uses it in relating an incident on 8 April 1940, when a section of Hurricanes of 43 Squadron (in which Peter was a flight commander) destroyed two Heinkel 111s in the late evening. He shot one down into the sea. On returning to base at Wick (the north-east tip of Scotland) he was told not to land on the flarepath as there was a crashed Heinkel in the middle of it. Short of fuel he landed to one side. This second Heinkel had been shot-up by Peter's number two (Hallowes), had made for the coast, seen the flarepath, and belly-landed on Wick. The unhurt German crew had insisted they had been attacked by Spitfires, although there was not one within miles. In mid May Peter Townsend was given command of 85 Squadron (Hurricanes), whose record throughout the Battle of Britain proved his ability not only as a fine fighter pilot but also as an outstanding leader. Like the rest of us, he had his anxious moments: into the sea a couple of times and a bullet in the foot. But let it be stated immediately that the combined total of several of us would not compare with my friend Al Deere's multitude of mishaps which he so modestly discards in the book.

At the beginning of this book I recalled incidents from 1940. Now, in the Epilogue, memory still holds the key, but my final thoughts are of people.

J.A.F. Maclachlan

Colin Grey Paddy Barthropp

In the Prologue, I told of the two Hurricanes which converged on the same enemy target, collided, and one pilot baled out. That pilot was Gordon Sinclair. He landed in Caterham (Surrey) outside the Guards Depot, at the feet of an officer who regarded him as he sat surrounded by parachute entanglements, and said: 'Hullo, Gordon, what are *you* doing here?' They had been at school together. I saw Gordon in Hyde Park a few days ago. He hadn't changed.

A happy thing about people is that their near-fatal experiences are always the subject of mirth to their friends and indeed to themselves in hindsight.

Duncan Smith, whose record as a fighter pilot covered most of the war, waited until he was a Group Captain in 1944 during the Italian campaign to be shot down in the Tyrrhenian Sea. He spent several hours in his dinghy in a hot sun before being picked up by the air-sea rescue. Cocky Dundas who saw him soon after the rescue said, 'He was all pink, just like a shrimp.'

I remember also Norman Ryder, another exceptional fighter pilot, of 41 Squadron (Spitfires). After being a bit careless over a convoy off Newcastle, he found himself too low to bale out and had to ditch his Spitfire in a sea which became rougher the nearer he got. The beautifully streamlined fighter slid into the water and continued downwards. As Norman said afterwards: 'The green turned to brown and then black and then I managed to get out. It seemed a long way to the surface.' In 1942, Norman Ryder, Bob Stanford Tuck, and I found ourselves with other rough characters in a German P.O.W. camp in Silesia.

The Royal Air Force seems to breed unusual characters. When I first took over 242 Squadron in June 1940, I encountered Pilot Officer Percival Stanley Turner. When Air Vice Marshal Leigh Mallory had given me the job, he had warned me that the squadron was composed mainly of Canadians. They'd had a rough time in France; they lacked a squadron commander and both flight commanders; they were tough, ill-disciplined, and bloody-minded. With his final exhortation 'Good luck' I hastened to Coltishall, in Norfolk, on my new assignment. I arrived late at night and made contact with the pilots of 242 early the next morning. Leigh Mallory had understated the situation. After my initial shock, I had my adjutant Peter Macdonald (a World War I veteran and Member of Parliament for the Isle of Wight) assemble all the pilots in my office. I then told them in reasonable words (or so I thought) how members of a good squadron should dress, behave, and generally conduct themselves. Having finished, I asked if anyone had anything to say. There was silence. Then a strong Canadian voice commented 'Horse-shit'. After a long pause, the same voice added 'Sir'. For some reason which even now I cannot define, this made the monstrously insubordinate interjection from Stan Turner entirely acceptable.

Stan was simply one of those people who was 'agin' authority'.

J.K. Quill
Right: 'Mutt' Summers

Denis Crowley-Milling

Dicky Cork   Jimmy Gardner

Barrie Heath

Any suggestion from a senior officer was automatically resisted, and then carried out loyally and thoroughly. We became life-long friends. After a magnificent war-time career, not entirely free from incident (depending on whether the particular senior officer he'd just insulted knew him or not), Stan ended the war a much-decorated Group Captain. He fought in both the Hurricane and Spitfire with equal ability. He is now president of a Canadian corporation.

Another fine Canadian, older than most of us and who fought in the Battle of Britain with distinction, was the late Gordon MacGregor who for many years after the war was President of Trans-Canada (now Air Canada). Others like Ernie MacNab, Dal Russell, Paul Davoud, were fighter pilots bred in the tradition of those great Canadians of World War I, Bishop, Barker, Collishaw and Carter. Australians like Clive 'Killer' Caldwell. New Zealanders like Al Deere, Colin Grey, Jamie Jamieson, 'Hawk-Eye' Wells and the great A.O.C. of 11 Group, Keith Park. South Africans, 'Sailor' Malan, Piet Hugo, Pat Pattle. Rhodesians like Johnnie Plagis, Ian Smith (now Premier), Bill Harper, Caesar Hull (with Peter Townsend in 43 Squadron—he died in the Battle of Britain). . . .

The list of names goes on and on, and this book must end. One final tribute must be paid to those two wonderful fighters, the Spitfire and the Hurricane. It is this. Many of us who flew them and fought in them believe that they had a lasting influence on our characters. They certainly affected our lives.

With the end of the Hitler War and the advent of the jet fighter a new era in military aviation had arrived. The day of the Spitfire and Hurricane was past. The Spitfire stayed some years longer with the Royal Air Force. Then it was gradually replaced by the subsonic Meteor and Vampire.

Nevertheless a number of foreign air forces continued to use not only these two British fighters but also their old opponent the Messerschmitt 109. On the credit titles of war films made in the 1950s and later were to be found phrases like, 'Hurricanes for this film were lent by the Portuguese Air Force'.

When the Battle of Britain film was made in 1968 the producers used German aircraft still flown by the Spanish Air Force, and they were flown by Spanish Air Force pilots. Every boy of twelve years of age—and almost none of the ex Battle of Britain pilots —seemed to notice that the Me 109s in this film were equipped with Rolls Royce Merlin engines. After 1945 the Spanish Air Force had been unable to obtain a Daimler Benz engine for their 109 so they got the Rolls Royce Merlin instead. It is ironical that the great German fighter made by Messerschmitt ended its life powered by the same Rolls Royce engine as its victorious opponent the Spitfire. *Sic transit gloria . . .*

Great Pilots of Polish Squadrons

Top: *W. A. Urbanowicz, who won the British D.F.C. and the Polish equivalent of the Victoria Cross*

Centre: *S. F. Skalski, who flew in Poland and France before joining the R.A.F.*

Bottom: *R. G. Kellett, who led the famous 303 Squadron*

Sonnet to a Windsock

Brave canvas on a thousand breezes borne,
Now on some scrapheap destined to be thrown,
By bullets riddled, and bomb splinters torn,
These fateful months you faithfully have flown.
For bloodshot eyes within the circuit flying,
The wind's own eye precisely you have found;—
Young men—and some are hurt and some are dying,—
At ninety knots they glide from air to ground.
Towards you my vizored friends, with one last glance,
Unleashed their Merlins—took off into cloud,
James fell in flames and Christopher in France,
For Peter and for Simon sea was shroud.
Shall 'danger-money' workmen end your year?
'Give it me please'! Young voices fill my ear.

W. D. O'HANLON Chaplain at Biggin Hill 1940–1942

December, 1940   R.A.F. Biggin Hill
The Works Department at the end of the year
replaced the Windsock at the shattered North End of
Biggin Hill Airfield. Fifty yards away is the Bomb
Shelter where forty W.A.A.F. were killed

A postscript and a final
tribute
Pilots of the Royal
Canadian Air Force, Royal
Australian Air Force,
Royal New Zealand Air
Force, Royal South African
Air Force, and United
States Air Force flew
Hurricanes and Spitfires
with distinction throughout
the war on all battle fronts.
Indeed, a USAF pilot, with
commendable modesty, is
reported as having said:
'The best combination was
a Yank in a Spitfire'.

INDEX

ACKNOWLEDGEMENTS

A.P., 66-7, 162-3
Bilderdienst, 20, 22-3, 26 (bottom), 30-1, 54, 56-7, 64-5, 96 (inset), 98-9, 114 (bottom)
B.A.C., 39 (bottom), 167 (top) 2
Bippa, 152-3
Camera Press, 53, 150-1, 157
Daily Mirror, 111 (inset)
Flight, 34-5, 37, 39 (centre), 40, 44
Fox Photos, 18, 28-9, 42, 70, 96-7, 97 (inset), 99 (inset)
Stewart Galloway, 146 (right)
Greyhound Racing Association, 133
Harrison, P., 119 (right)
Hawker Siddeley, 145 (right), 168
I.W.M., 2-3, 6, 10-11, 13, 14, 17, 28-9 (inset), 38, 39 (top), 47, 48-9, 55, 58, 61 (inset), 62-3, 74-5, 90, 98 (inset), 100-1, 102-3, 106 (top), 112-13, 114-15, (top), 115 (bottom), 116, 121, 122-3, 127, 128, 132, 134-5, 139, 140-1, 142-3 (bottom), 144, 149, 160-1, 166 (top 2)
Kent Messenger, 8, 24 (bottom), 26 (top), 60-1
Keystone, 24 (centre), 72-3, 74-5, 104, 142-3 (top), 159, 160-1 (top)
Ministry of Defence, 59
Natkiel, Richard, 79 (map)
Popperfoto, 51
Royal Navy, 137 (right)
Sport and General, 166 (bottom)
Topix, 94-5
Ullstein, 4-5, 24 (top), 27, 77, 106 (bottom), 108-9, 124-5
U.P.1., 110-11
Vickers, 1, 45

I.W.M. = by courtesy of the Trustees of the Imperial War Museum:

I would like to commend the following publications which have helped me: *Spitfire—the story of a famous fighter* by Bruce Robertson; *The Hawker Hurricane* by Francis K. Mason; *Full Circle* by Johnnie Johnson; *Nine Lives* by Alan C. Deere; *Aces High* by Shores and Williams; *Famous Air Battles* by John Frayn Turner; *The Royal Air Force* 1939-45 HMSO; *The Battle of Britain* HMSO; *The Air Battle of Malta* HMSO; *We Speak from the Air* HMSO; *Over to You* HMSO.

The colour photographs between pages 80 and 89 are acknowledged as follows: the first three pages to the Imperial War Museum, the next three to the wartime magazine *Signal*, and the last two to the Conway Picture Library.